COMBAT AIRCRAFT

143 F3D/EF-10 SKYKNIGHT UNITS OF THE KOREAN AND VIETNAM WARS

SERIES EDITOR TONY HOLMES

143

COMBAT AIRCRAFT

Joe Copalman

F3D/EF-10 SKYKNIGHT UNITS OF THE KOREAN AND VIETNAM WARS

OSPREY
PUBLISHING

OSPREY PUBLISHING

Bloomsbury Publishing Plc

Kemp House, Chawley Park, Cumnor Hill, Oxford, OX2 9PH, UK

29 Earlsfort Terrace, Dublin 2, Ireland

1385 Broadway, 5th Floor, New York, NY 10018, USA

E-mail; info@ospreypublishing.com

www.ospreypublishing.com

OSPREY is a trademark of Osprey Publishing Ltd

First published in Great Britain in 2022

A catalogue record for this book is available from the British Library.

ISBN; PB 9781472846259; eBook 9781472846266; ePDF 9781472846235; XML 9781472846242

22 23 24 25 26   10 9 8 7 6 5 4 3 2 1

Edited by Tony Holmes
Cover Artwork by Gareth Hector
Aircraft Profiles by Jim Laurier
Index by Zoe Ross
Originated by PDQ Digital Media Solutions, UK
Printed and bound in India by Replika Press Private Ltd

Osprey Publishing supports the Woodland Trust, the UK's leading woodland conservation charity.

FSC
MIX
Paper from responsible sources
FSC® C016779
www.fsc.org

To find out more about our authors and books visit **www.ospreypublishing.com**. Here you will find extracts, author interviews, details of forthcoming events and the option to sign up for our newsletter.

Front Cover

Although an EW platform, the EF-10B Skyknight carried a K-17 reconnaissance camera in the rear fuselage. In August 1966, EF-10 crews from VMCJ-1 at Da Nang detected a 'Cross Slot' early warning radar just north of the DMZ separating North and South Vietnam. To accurately fix the radar's position for an air strike, crews needed reconnaissance photographs of the site. Seventh Air Force – which ran the air war from Saigon – restricted US Marine Corps photo-reconnaissance aircraft from flying north of the DMZ, meaning VMCJ-1's RF-8A Crusaders could not verify the 'Cross Slot's' location. Maj Jim Doyle, an ECMO from VMCJ-1, serving as the US Marine Corps liaison officer to Seventh Air Force, 'fragged' an EF-10B sortie north of the DMZ, notionally to gather electronic intelligence. Unaware that the EF-10B also carried a camera, the USAF approved the mission.

On 24 August, 1Lts Gail Sublett (pilot) and H Wayne Whitten (ECMO) flew the special photo-reconnaissance mission in EF-10B BuNo 125869, passing over the suspected radar site at 10,000 ft and taking photogaphs. Sublett and Whitten then agreed on a second pass at low altitude to try and visually acquire the radar. Flying slightly above treetop level, they drew fire from several AAA guns and automatic weapons, with their 'Whale' taking a round from the latter through its nose.

Sublett and Whitten's photos confirmed the radar's location, which led to Seventh Air Force approving a RF-8 mission by VMCJ-1 to photograph the site. With targeting-quality imagery for strike planning, US Marine Corps F-4 Phantom II and F-8 Crusader crews flew a mission against the site, destroying the 'Cross Slot'. The operation was executed entirely by MAG-11 crews and aircraft, and demonstrated what VMCJ-1 brought to the fight (Cover artwork by Gareth Hector)

PREVIOUS PAGES

With the Skyknight in high demand for ECM escort over North Vietnam, 1st MAW restricted 'Whale' pilots from using its twin 20 mm cannon in air-to-ground work. Despite this, a VMCJ-1 EF-10B pilot made two known strafing passes against North Vietnamese targets. The Skyknights retained two cannon for last-ditch self-defence, with pilots routinely test-firing them en route to North Vietnam – hence the cannon residue on BuNo 127051's inboard gun ports. The two outboard gun ports were empty (Jim Sullivan Collection)

Acknowledgements

My sincere thanks to BGen Art Bloomer, Col H Wayne Whitten, Lt Cols Hugh Tom Carter, Dave Foss and Charles Houseman, Majs Jim Doyle and Len Ingram, Capt Al Olsen, Terry Whalen, Ben Kristy at NMMC, Ed Neglovski and Nancy Whitfield at USMC History Division, Danny Stevens at NHHC, Bob Thomas at NNAM, Takis Diakoumis, Peter Greengrass, Hal and Ted Barker from the Korean War Project and Dr Steve Maxner at the Texas Tech Vietnam Center and Archive. Thanks to Mark Aldrich, Paul Bless, Richard Burgess, Ron Picciani, Jim Sullivan and Warren Thompson for imagery – photographs on previous pages and pg 67 Fritz Gemeinhardt, courtesy Jim Sullivan; photos pgs 6, 10, 12, 13, 14, 20, 23, 26, 29 Charles Trask, courtesy Jim Sullivan; photos pgs 8, 19, 46 (bottom) Eugene Holmberg, courtesy Tailhook Association; photo pg 57 Bill Swisher, courtesy Tailhook Association. Finally, thank you to my wife Jonna and children Nora and James.

CONTENTS

CHAPTER ONE

SKYKNIGHTS OVER KOREA

The Douglas F3D Skyknight entered service in December 1950 as the US Navy and US Marine Corps' first carrier-based jet nightfighter. Given the demanding specifications for what became the Skyknight, the design, by Ed Heinemann, was surprisingly conventional, with straight wings, low-profile engine nacelles tucked in close to the fuselage and a tail that looked more at home on a World War 2-era medium bomber than a jet fighter.

The F3D featured a wide fuselage to incorporate the Westinghouse AN/APQ-35 radar system, consisting of two different radars mounted in tandem in the Skyknight's cavernous nosecone. Installed at the rear of the nosecone was the large dish for the AN/APS-21 search radar, used for detecting and tracking targets, with the smaller AN/APG-26 gun-laying radar dish mounted in front of it. Under optimal conditions, the AN/APS-21 could detect targets up to 20 miles away, while the AN/APG-26 could lock on to targets up to 2.25 miles ahead. Additionally, the Skyknight carried an AN/APS-28 tail warning radar with a ten-mile detection range – a system that would prove critical in the dark skies over North Korea.

Shortly after accepting its first Skyknights, the US Marine Corps began preparing its initial cadre of F3D pilots, radar operators (ROs) and maintainers for service in the Korean War. The unit chosen to receive the jet was Marine All-Weather Fighter Squadron (VMF(N)) 542, which

A well-weathered F3D-2 from VMF(N)-513 'Flying Nightmares' flies just above a solid undercast over South Korea. The unit proved the Skyknight's prowess as a nightfighter with a 6-to-1 kill ratio (*Jim Sullivan Collection*)

departed Kimpo, in South Korea, in March 1951 and returned to Marine Corps Air Station (MCAS) El Toro, in California, for conversion from the F7F Tigercat to the F3D-1.

Following more than a year of instruction on the new jet, air- and groundcrews trained on the Skyknight would head back to South Korea with 15 improved F3D-2s. This model featured more powerful Westinghouse J34-WE-36 turbojet engines, each rated at 3400 lb st (the D-1 had been fitted with J34-WE-32s of 3000 lb st), a bulletproof windscreen, an autopilot and a few additional upgrades.

Once in-theatre, the aircraft and their crews would join the 'Flying Nightmares' of VMF(N)-513. The latter had already been deployed for more than a year, flying the F4U-5N Corsair and F7F Tigercat on night ground attack missions and combat air patrols (CAPs).

The F3D cadre commenced its journey to South Korea on 27 May 1952 when an advance party led by Col Peter D Lambrecht departed El Toro for K-8 air base near Kunsan to begin the Skyknight bed-down process with VMF(N)-513, arriving on 1 June after a quick stop in Japan. The remainder of the F3D cadre reached Yokosuka, in Japan, on 18 June, with 15 jets being transported to a nearby Naval Air Station at Kisarazu. Here, groundcrew prepared each aircraft for the short hop to Itami air base, where the Skyknights underwent further preparation for the flight to Kunsan. The remaining US Marine Corps personnel departed for Kunsan to prepare for the arrival of the aircraft.

The first cadre of US Marine Corps Skyknight pilots, ROs and maintainers trained on F3D-1s with VMF(N)-542 at MCAS El Toro in southern California between March 1951 and April 1952. Just 28 'Dash Ones' were built by Douglas, including this aircraft, BuNo 123757. It had briefly served with US Navy unit VC-3 prior to being passed on to VMF(N)-542 (*Tailhook Association*)

While at Itami, the Skyknights had their Glossy Sea Blue scheme painted over with flat black, while the high-visibility unit markings were replaced by dull red stencilling. It was hoped that this change in schemes would reduce the enemy's ability to visually acquire the F3D in the night skies over North Korea.

Of the 15 aircraft shipped to Japan, the cadre took 12 to South Korea, with Col Lambrecht leading the first flight of four Skyknights from Itami to K-8 on 24 June. The F3D cadre jumped right into local operations from Kunsan, with the first test and area familiarisation flights taking place the day after the jets' arrival. By the 27th, all 12 aircraft had reached K-8.

Unfortunately, the Skyknights would not be able to fly combat missions over North Korea for several months, as the cadre deployed without the gun barrel extensions required to fire the four M2 20 mm cannon that were the aircraft's only armament. The 'Nightmares' continued to restrict the F3D to local flights throughout July 1952, keeping crews busy with area familiarisation, test flying and night intercept training to build proficiency utilising the APQ-35 radar system.

The squadron finally received the first five sets of gun barrel extensions on 5 August. Installation was completed and a test flight the following day confirmed the weapons functioned properly. During the course of the month, VMF(N)-513 accepted 16 more sets of barrel extensions. With a growing fleet of combat-ready aircraft, the unit soon began sending armed jets into the night sky for live missions.

The first operational F3D mission in Korea had not been planned as such. Royal Air Force exchange pilot Sqn Ldr John R Gardener and his US Marine Corps RO SSgt Kropp had been on a local air intercept training

The Skyknight's Westinghouse AN/APQ-35 radar system consisted of the AN/APS-21 search radar and AN/APG-26 targeting radar, with the antenna dishes arranged in tandem order in the aircraft's spacious nose. The larger dish of the AN/APS-21 is seen here at the rear, while the much smaller dish for the AN/APG-26 is mounted forward of it (*Tailhook Association*) sortie on the night of 7 August when a ground controller diverted them to search for an aircraft squawking an emergency identification friend or foe (IFF) code. While orbiting in the area they had been vectored to, the controller informed them the aircraft in question was not actually in distress after all.

Before entering the war in earnest, all Skyknight crews met for a briefing on 9 August with a trio of controllers from 'Dentist', the ground-controlled intercept (GCI) site on Ch'o-do Island (off the west coast of North Korea) that they would be working with for night combat air patrol (NCAP) missions. The briefers laid out the coordination procedures for F3D pilots preparing to fly operationally under their control. Conversely, the 'Nightmares' sent three officers to Ch'o-do to observe controllers working live intercepts in order to give the squadron a better understanding of what they saw on their scopes.

Col Lambrecht and his RO, 2Lt James Brown, flew the first NCAP mission on 11 August, orbiting north of Ch'o-do before being vectored north along the North Korean coast. The flight was uneventful, with no contacts or intercepts made. The next evening, Maj James Martin and his RO, MSgt Thompson, received a vector from 'Dentist' toward an unidentified aircraft. As they closed with the bogey, they encountered enemy jamming of their AN/APS-21 radar, likely from a ground station inside North Korea, and 'Dentist' called off the intercept. Three hours later, Maj Harold Eiland and MSgt Piekutowski encountered the same jamming in a nearby area.

Throughout August, the 'Nightmares' learned first-hand the challenges crews faced when hunting the enemy in the dark. Given the limits of the technology at the time, ROs commonly received solid vectors from GCI

F3D-2 crews from VMF(N)-513 pose in front of a 'Nightmares'' Skyknight at Kunsan in this autumn 1952 photograph. The first F3D-2s had arrived at K-8 on 24 June 1952, and they were flown alongside VMF(N)-513's F4U-5N Corsairs and F7F-3N Tigercats – an example of the latter is parked to the left of the Skyknight (*Tailhook Association*)

operators to contacts they failed to detect themselves on radar in the jet. Conversely, Skyknight crews sometimes reported seeing navigation lights from aircraft the GCI controllers had never detected. But even when the aerial and ground-based systems worked together, the process of closing with, identifying and locking up an enemy aircraft with the AN/APG-26 proved difficult.

Describing such an encounter in August 1952, Capt Lyle B Matthews Jr wrote;

'We were given a vector to intercept a bogey at approximately [grid location] YC 1065. At the time, we had 4800 lbs of fuel remaining and we were flying at 30,000 ft indicated. A head-on run was set up by "Dentist" but no joy. We then followed the bogey on an approximate rectangular course, which seemed to be centred over the position being worked by "Flytrain 35" [F7F Tigercats flying night interdiction] and "Fatface" [a US Navy PB4Y-2 Privateer flareship] below. We kept requesting lower altitudes from "Dentist", until at an altitude of 11,000 ft we were informed that the bogey's "angels" were 20 [altitude of 20,000 ft]. Thirty seconds later, we had an airborne target on our gear at eight miles. When assured that the contact was

Delivered without the gun tube extensions for the Skyknight's four 20 mm cannon, 'Nightmare' F3D-2s (including BuNo 124608, seen here breaking away from its flight lead) were initially restricted to local familiarisation and post-maintenance test flights in the Kunsan area from late June through to early August 1952 (*Jim Sullivan Collection*) solid, we gave a "Roger Dee" [code acknowledging radar lock-up on "Dentist's" intended contact].

'We then set up a climb at 240 [knots] indicated, which gave us a slight overtaking speed. At one-and-a-half miles, we attempted a lock-on, and found that our [AN/APG-]26 antenna was stuck in the up position. We then closed to minimum range on the AN/APS-21 gear – about 1000 ft – but I was unable to obtain a visual on the bogey. We were synchronised behind the bogey for about three minutes, with no visual obtained. We then proceeded through minimum range at a slight overtaking speed, but at about that time the bogey must have turned to a southerly heading, for our next report from "Dentist" had the contact at "nine o'clock" at eight miles.'

In addition to the occasional MiG-15 nightfighter, Skyknight pilots also faced the far more common threat of high-calibre anti-aircraft artillery (AAA). Radar-guided searchlights could turn night into day, illuminating even high-flying F3Ds enough to give gunners adequate visibility to lead their targets. A common tactic the enemy employed was setting traps for American nightfighters by using a MiG as 'bait', the jet flying straight and level with its navigation lights on, tempting Skyknight pilots to give chase. Working in concert with Chinese GCI, the 'bait' MiG led kill-hungry F3D crews into well-constructed ambushes, with enemy gunners waiting in the dark below.

Capt Dean Caswell was one of the first F3D pilots to encounter such a trap during an NCAP on 15 August. Detailing this encounter for the squadron's command diary, he recalled;

'I was vectored by "Dentist" onto a bandit in the Antung area. I believe the bandit was a jet-type aircraft by vectors and speed indicated. Four miles southeast of Antung, I observed three bright arc-type lights in a line running northwest to southeast, estimated to be one half-mile apart. These lights stayed on for two minutes. As these lights went off, four batteries of two searchlights each came on in a five-mile radius west of Antung. Those lights picked me up. I believed I was mouse-trapped and evaded the lights immediately.'

The same night Caswell encountered the searchlight trap, the squadron experienced its first loss. Col Lambrecht and his RO, 2Lt James M Brown, departed Kunsan for an NCAP mission and simply failed to return. The squadron sent up an F4U-5N to search Lambrecht's last known position, followed by two F7Fs, but none of the crews spotted any fire, wreckage or evidence of the aircraft. Despite the tremendous blow to squadron morale caused by the loss of a well-liked commanding officer so early into a combat tour, the Skyknight crews continued their nightly vigils near Ch'o-do.

FIRST TAIL RADAR HIT

Of the three radars equipping the F3D-2, the AN/APS-28 tail warning unit proved to be the aircraft's 'ace-in-the-hole'. Although Skyknight crews routinely received timely warning from GCI controllers of rear-quarter threats approaching during NCAP missions, the AN/APS-28 gave pilots and ROs a level of autonomy the enemy lacked when it came to threat awareness.

The first operational 'hit' on a bogey from the AN/APS-28 occurred on 22 August when Capt Robert E Paulson and his RO detected an unknown aircraft with the tail warning unit while on a night CAP mission. Paulson remarked in the squadron's command diary;

"At 2340 hrs "Flytrain 3388", on a heading of 220 degrees in the vicinity of [grid location] XD 5053, picked up a bogey indication on the tail warning gear. Distance of contact was one mile, and it appeared to be 5000 ft above. "Flytrain" was at 29,000 ft at time. Distance of contact increased rapidly as though the bogey contact was travelling in the opposite direction. "Flytrain 3388" turned 180 degrees back to the vicinity of the first contact. Again, a contact was picked up on the tail warning gear. Search on [AN/]APS-21 gear proved negative. No more contacts.'

The 'Nightmares' began September with another F3D loss on the night of the 1st. Unlike the disappearance of Lambrecht and Brown less than three weeks prior, this loss resulted in a nearly two-month stand-down as the US Marine Corps attempted to identify why the Skyknights were crashing, and how to resolve it. This mishap was unusual because it had something most Skyknight losses in Korea (and Vietnam, for that matter) did not – a survivor.

The F3D featured a chute through which the pilot and RO could escape, rather than ejection seats, which were still rare at the time. With this mishap occurring at relatively low altitude, the chute was not an option – pilot Maj Harrold J Eiland and RO MSgt Alois A Motil went in with the aircraft. By some twist of fate, Motil found himself free of the wreckage after the jet crashed into the ocean, and he was picked up by a rescue boat about an hour later. Recounting the mishap in the 'Nightmares' September 1952 command diary, Motil wrote;

'On starting engines, the port engine started normally but the starboard engine took an excessive amount of cranking before starting. Everything checked out normally and radio contact with the tower was established. At

The frayed ends of the aluminium matting on this refuelling pad give a good idea of the conditions Skyknights operated under in Korea, at both K-8 (Kunsan) and K-6 (Pyongtaek). As with all F3D-2s in-theatre, BuNo 124620 carried an APS-28 tail warning radar that was capable of giving the RO range and altitude information on contacts up to ten miles behind the aircraft. The APS-28 proved invaluable to Skyknight crews flying both NCAP and B-29 escort missions over North Korea (*Jim Sullivan Collection*)

The 'Flying Nightmares' stencilled red 'nightcap' markings beneath the cockpits of their jets as a visual reminder of just how many combat missions had been flown by each aircraft. 'WF 1' in the foreground was clearly a dependable airframe (*Jim Sullivan Collection*)

approximately 0139/l [hrs] we were given take-off clearance and proceeded with a normal take-off. Halfway down the runway, the port engine lost about ten per cent rpm, which was apparently corrected by the action of the pilot. Shortly thereafter, the starboard engine gave a slight drop in rpm, but immediately returned to normal. A fluctuation of power in the engines, such as this, has never been experienced by me on my previous flights in this type of aircraft.

'We continued the take-off on a heading of 240 degrees and made a normal climb-out. After approximately three or four minutes, and when in the overcast at what I thought to be about 3000 ft altitude, we experienced an explosion in the starboard engine, accompanied by a blinding light, similar to lightning, and a clanging noise indicative of metal on metal. The fire warning light did not come on at any time, nor did the tachometer indicate any drop in rpm. Both fire warning lights had been checked prior to take-off.

'When the right wing dropped, the pilot took corrective action. Immediately thereafter, a second explosion took place, this time in the left engine. It was similar in all respects to the first one. At no time did the Major go off the gauges. I turned my head towards the pilot and attempted to contact him on the ICS [inter communication system] but the radio was out. As I turned my head to the radar scope, we experienced a third blinding explosion, at which time I could feel the tail of the aircraft come up violently, similar to a somersault. I can remember my head being down pointed towards the windscreen.

'About that time, I seemed to be floating free in the water, although my safety belt and shoulder harness were cinched tight prior to take-off. As I gained consciousness, I found myself treading water.'

After an hour in the water, Motil saw lights from a rescue boat in the distance. Although injured, he managed to fire several signal flares, and the rescue boat arrived at his location. Once aboard, Motil inquired about Maj Eiland, and the crew replied they had not located him yet. With his injuries not life-threatening, Motil asked the crew to keep looking and the crew complied, continuing their search, eventually returning to Kunsan harbour due to tidal conditions.

As a result of this mishap, the US Marine Corps prohibited F3Ds from combat missions, effective 1 September. Given MSgt Motil's recollection of the mishap, investigators suspected the third stage of the turbine compressor in the port engine had failed, shedding compressor blades into the interior of the aircraft – a failure suspected in the loss of other F3Ds in the US. Throughout September, the 'Nightmares' waited on armour shielding for the third stage of the J34 turbine compressor. In the meantime, the squadron received authorisation on 6 September to conduct local VFR test flights. The unit finally received the new compressor shields on 17 October. The maintainers installed enough shields for Skyknights to begin flying operational missions again, with NCAPs over Ch'o-do resuming on the night of 18 October.

Following all the frustrations of the first few months of F3D operations in Korea, VMF(N)-513 hit the ground running in November. In addition to continuing the nightly Ch'o-do NCAPs, the squadron eagerly fulfilled a request from the USAF to escort B-29 bombers on night raids over North Korea. This new mission provided VMF(N)-513 with the opportunity to prove the F3D in combat against enemy aircraft at night. Under the leadership of Lt Col Homer G Hutchinson – a particularly aggressive pilot who assumed command on 9 September – the squadron also began

After some initial struggles with maintenance and supply – particularly a shortage of vacuum tubes for the F3D's three radars – VMF(N)-513's maintainers and avionics Marines developed practices that kept the squadron's Skyknights in fighting shape for the remainder of the war. In an expeditionary environment plagued by challenging weather extremes, this was no small feat (*Jim Sullivan Collection*) racking up ground kills against targets of opportunity, with Hutchinson leading the way.

While the US Navy and US Marine Corps had both obtained the F3D for night and all-weather air intercept missions, in the summer of 1952, Navy Composite Squadron (VC) 33 evaluated the Skyknight's suitability as a night ground attack platform and concluded it was better suited to counter-air operations. Regardless, Hutchinson put the Skyknight's guns to work against enemy trucks for the first time on 2 November while heading back from an uneventful NCAP mission. Hutchinson made a strafing pass against a column of vehicles on one of the main supply routes (MSRs) running north-to-south in North Korea, expending 150 rounds of 20 mm ammunition and damaging two trucks in the process.

Two nights later, Capt Robert Parnell and his RO, TSgt Smith, flew an NCAP mission, during which the only bogey 'Dutchboy' GCI vectored them onto turned out to be a B-29 heading back to Japan. On their return to Kunsan, Parnell dropped to low altitude to strafe a North Korean factory, putting 360 rounds of 20 mm shells into it with no observable effects. The day after Lt Col Hutchinson's impromptu interdiction of two communist trucks, VMF(N)-513 flew its first bomber escort mission.

USAF B-29 Stratofortresses played a central role in the strategic bombing campaign against North Korea. However, they had taken such a battering at the hands of communist MiG-15s by the autumn of 1951 that Far East Air Force (FEAF) Bomber Command switched the B-29s to night missions only. While shifting to night operations reduced losses compared to those suffered during daylight missions, many dangers awaited the bombers in the dark. Radar-guided searchlights proved especially effective at ensnaring B-29s for engagement by AAA and MiG-15s, which – while not equipped with on-board radar to target bombers in complete darkness – relied on skilled GCI controllers to guide them into optimal firing positions against the lumbering bombers.

By mid-1952, the USAF had found the right combination of radar jamming and chaff deployment to mitigate the searchlight and AAA threat. The MiGs, however, continued to hunt the B-29s, scoring a major victory over the bombers on 10 June when they downed two aircraft from the 19th Bombardment Group (BG) over Kwaksan, damaging a third one so extensively that it never flew again after making an emergency landing at Kimpo. The Superfortress crews needed 'nocturnal linebackers' to protect them from the MiG threat.

The USAF had a capable nightfighter in the Lockheed F-94B Starfire – a development of the T-33 Shooting Star with the addition of an afterburner and a Hughes E-1 Fire Control System. The E-1 was fitted in both the Starfire and the Northrop F-89 Scorpion, the USAF's two frontline interceptors at the time tasked primarily with defending North America from Soviet nuclear bombers. The E-1 consisted of the A-1C gunsight and the AN/APG-33 radar, the latter being a development of the AN/APG-3, which outfitted Strategic Air Command's Convair B-36 'Peacemaker' nuclear bomber.

Just as the USAF deliberately chose to commit its comparatively ancient B-29s to missions over North Korea to prevent frontline bombers with the most recent technology from falling into communist hands in the event of a shootdown, the F-94 was restricted to defensive NCAPs over South Korea, lest the Soviets acquire any insights into how the E-1 worked and how to defeat it. With the Starfire out of consideration and the F3D's capabilities being proven during NCAP missions, the 'Flying Nightmares' became the best option for B-29 escort, and the unit was happy to commit to it.

The first B-29 escort mission occurred on 3 November, with Lt Col Jack Scott and TSgt Scott (no relation) flying as 'Volleyball 35' and reporting negative contacts throughout the mission.

Whereas NCAP missions involved flying to a specific area and awaiting vectors to bogeys from the Ch'o-do GCI site, escorting B-29s demanded significantly more planning and preparation. US Navy Lt G G 'Jerry' O'Rourke, an F3D pilot who commanded a detachment of four F3Ds and five aircrews that would attach to VMF(N)-513 during June and July 1953, offered the following insights into escort preparation in his book *Night Fighters Over Korea*;

'The B-29 escort operation was massive, to say the least. They required extensive briefings, a lot of study of charts and tables, extremely careful navigation, unbelievably intense in-flight coordination between aircraft, and a truly professional pilot–RO team in every F3D cockpit.'

A typical B-29 escort mission involved a minimum of six Skyknights. Two provided barrier CAP, orbiting to the north between the bomber stream and the MiG sanctuaries in China to prevent interlopers from attacking from that direction. Another two orbited the initial point for the bombers and escorted them from there to the target to deal with any MiGs that made it past the barrier CAP. Two more escorted the bombers from the target out of North Korea. Typically, at least one more Skyknight flew the target CAP position, orbiting over the target to engage any threats waiting to ambush the approaching or egressing bombers.

A common claim made about the 'Nightmares' in Korea states that no B-29s were lost while under escort by F3Ds from the unit. However, the USAF did lose a few Superfortresses to MiGs after the US Marine Corps committed Skyknights to the escort mission. Such was the case on the night of 18–19 November 1952 when B-29 44-86392 *Wrights' Delights* of the 98th Bombardment Wing's 345th Bombardment Squadron (BS) fell victim to MiG-15s after dropping its bombs on a target in Songhon, North Korea. Although all 14 crew bailed out of the burning bomber, only two survived, the others being either listed as missing or killed in action – proof of just how costly the loss of a single bomber could be.

The 'Nightmares' struck back on 3 November, when Maj William Stratton and MSgt Hans Hoglind claimed the first victory for the F3D while on an NCAP mission. In the November 1952 VMF(N)-513 command diary, Stratton wrote;

'At approximately 0107/I [hrs] at 14,000 ft, contact was made on radar. Unidentified at same altitude heading approximately 330 degrees, speed 320 knots, distance seven miles. Contact lost, then again established, same

The 'Flying Nightmares' scored the first jet-on-jet kill at night when Maj William Stratton and MSgt Hans Hoglind downed what they believed to be a Yak-15 on the night of 2–3 November 1952. Regardless of the type of aircraft, the kill energised VMF(N)-513 and validated its tactics. Stratton and Hoglind are seen here in front of 'WF 23', the aircraft they scored their kill in. Incidentally, Lt Col Robert Conley and MSgt James Scott flew this same aircraft when they shot down a MiG-15 on 31 January 1953 (*Paul Bless Collection*)

distance. Closed to 2100 ft. [AN/]APG-26 would not lock, visual sighting made of single-engined jet-type aircraft identified as Yak-15 at 0110 [hrs]. After some delay, permission was given by "Dutchboy" (Ch'o-do GCI) to "bag bandit". Opened fire at approximately 0113 [hrs] at 12,000 ft altitude, 1200 ft from directly astern. First burst hit port wing of bandit, second fuselage, third entered tailpipe, exploding therein. Three explosions in all were observed, and plane smoked heavily as it went down. Last seen at 6000 ft still on fire and smoking.'

The specific jet type noted in Stratton's account has been called into question over the years, most notably by Professor Richard P Hallion, who posited in his 1986 book *The Naval Air War Over Korea* that with the Yak-15 being a daylight type never encountered over North Korea prior to or following the shootdown, Stratton and Hoglind likely downed a Yak-17, which the Russians used to train new Chinese jet pilots.

However, more recent Russian sources, relying on declassified Soviet records, claim the aircraft Stratton struck was a MiG-15 flown by Capt V D Vishnyak of the 147th Guards Fighter Aviation Regiment (IAP), and that Vishnyak managed to recover his stricken aircraft safely. Regardless of the type of aircraft hit, or its ultimate disposition, Stratton and Hoglind's kill energised the F3D crews, convincing them their tactics were sound and that the Skyknight worked as advertised. Just days later, the 'Nightmares' scored another kill.

In the early morning hours of 8 November 1952, 'Dutchboy' vectored Capt Oliver R Davis and WO Dramus 'Ding' Fessler onto a bogey that resulted in VMF(N)-513's second kill. Davis, in his command diary account, recalled;

'At 0132 [hrs], I was vectored 230 degrees by "Dutchboy", who notified me that a bogey was at "12 o'clock", ten miles, at 12,500 ft. I began a dive from 19,500 ft and added full power at 14,000 ft. "Dutchboy" radioed "heads up" because our blips were merged on his scope. My RO got the contact and ordered "gentle starboard". The contact was lost immediately, and I requested further help from "Dutchboy", who vectored me on a heading of 270 degrees and repeated that the bogey was at 12,500 ft altitude. My RO re-established contact with the bogey at "12 o'clock", three miles. He ordered a gentle starboard turn and I executed a 30-degree bank. We began closing at an indicated airspeed of 450 knots. My RO placed us in a position so that the bogey was ten degrees starboard, three miles, at 12,000 ft.

'As we closed, I got a visual on a jet exhaust. I requested "Dutchboy" to distinguish as to whether it was a "bogey" or a "bandit". He replied "Bag it, bag it". By then I was from a quarter- to a half-mile from the exhaust and closing rapidly. I momentarily popped the speed brakes. The exhaust was so bright it was hard for me to make out the airframe outline. The bandit began a hard turn to starboard, and I turned with him and fired a short burst of about 20 rounds of 20 mm into the tailpipe. There was an explosion and parts flew past my plane. I was closing dangerously. I pulled hard back on the stick, and since I was already in a hard starboard turn, I passed the enemy to his right. I observed flame and black smoke passing from the centre portion of his plane. After reversing my turn, I picked up a visual on the flaming craft as it descended and crashed. There was another explosion upon impact.'

Soviet records confirm the loss of a MiG-15 on that date, and identify the pilot as Lt Ivan P Kovalyov of the 351st Night Fighter Aviation Regiment. Yet another account holds that communist GCI controllers 'expertly' guided Kovalyov into an intentional mid-air collision, rather than a firing position, with an F-94 – an impossibility since FEAF did not clear Starfires for missions north of the bombline until mid-March 1953.

NCAPs CONTINUE

Despite taking on the additional commitment of the B-29 escorts, VMF(N)-513 remained committed to the nightly NCAP missions near Ch'o-do. A typical NCAP sortie lasted two hours, with each transit leg from Kunsan to Ch'o-do taking 30 minutes each way, giving crews one hour on station. While outbound from K-8, the pilot would request a 'parrot' check from a Tactical Air Coordination Center to verify his IFF transponder was working, while the RO did functional checks on the radar systems. If either system malfunctioned, the crew aborted the mission.

With a good 'parrot' and an 'up' radar, the pilot continued north, checking in with 'Dentist' (later callsigns for the Ch'o-do GCI site were 'Dutchboy', 'Kodak' and 'Mongoose') while 20 miles south of Ch'o-do,

The RO's instrument display on the righthand side of the F3D-2's cockpit (*Tailhook Association*)

before continuing to an orbit between 20 and 30 miles north of the island. From this orbit, a Skyknight crew could be vectored toward any bogeys flying the nightly patrol between Antung and Pyongyang. Whether vectored against a MiG or remaining in the orbit north of Ch'o-do, once the Skyknight's hour on station has passed, the pilot returned to K-8 to debrief the mission.

As the 'Nightmares' became more proficient with the aerial game of cat and mouse, the Chinese, North Korean and Russian MiG pilots – and their GCI controllers – learned to play the game as well. Although the extent to which the communists knew US forces employed radar-equipped fighters over North Korea at the time is unknown, one evasion tactic they frequently used worked just as well against aerial radars as it did against the distant American GCI sites. By diving for the deck, a MiG pilot could dip below Ch'o-do's radar coverage, while also masking his aircraft against the clutter of radar ground return. Maj Robert Conley encountered this tactic on an NCAP mission on 5 November, with MSgt Page in his right seat;

'Observed three airborne lights paralleling own course, same air speed, at 20,000 ft altitude. Requested information from "Dutchboy", and received vector. Radar contact made at six miles range. Bogey dived for deck, range increasing to six-and-one-half miles. Bogey lost in ground return, 12,000 ft altitude and still diving. Vectored again by "Dutchboy", contact established two miles range, target again lost in ground return.'

The communist pilots also became adept at using the MiG-15's superior speed and turn performance when engaged by F3Ds. On 6 November, Maj James Martin and MSgt Thompson received a vector from 'Dutchboy' to a contact north of Ch'o-do, with the bandit using his greater manoeuvrability to shake off the Skyknight. As Martin recalled;

'Received vector after bandit, made radar contact "12 o'clock", seven miles. Contact in ground return during a hard port turn. Pilot then observed an airborne light, apparently a jet exhaust. Chase begun, with three contacts made and lost on radar gear. A port vector was given by "Dutchboy", and intermittent contacts on bandit during hard turns made in an effort to close. Unable to turn inside of bandit. Intercept broken off due to lack of fuel.'

That same night, Maj William Stratton and MSgt Hans Hoglind, flying as 'Volleyball 38', encountered another MiG on an NCAP north of Ch'o-do. Their opponent simply accelerated away, denying them a second kill. In the squadron's command diary, Stratton noted;

'Vectored onto bogey, radar contact made 0130 [hrs], eight miles, showing above "Volleyball" at 12,000 ft altitude. Range decreased to four miles when contact was lost while in a hard starboard turn. "Dutchboy" continued vectors and reported range had opened to 12 miles and bogey had dropped to 6000 ft altitude. When friendly had reached 5000 ft altitude, indicated airspeed 480 knots, the intercept was broken off due to slow rate of closing speed and lack of fuel.'

In addition to the Chinese-based MiGs defending North Korea from US bombers, the North Korean People's Air Force employed aircraft with far lower performance against targets in South Korea. Operating exclusively at night, these light aircraft – primarily Polikarpov

Most 'Nightmare' aircrews flew as paired combat crews – set teams of pilots and ROs who flew missions together night after night. Here, one such team – RO MSgt Larry Fortin (left) and pilot Maj Jack Dunn (middle) – debrief with an intelligence officer after a mission (*Jim Sullivan Collection*)

Po-2 biplanes and, to a lesser extent, Yakovlev Yak-18s – sought to disrupt United Nations (UN) ground and air operations. While these 'night hecklers' were never the same threat to UN forces that B-29s or even B-26s were to the communists, a handful of these light, strategically-insignificant aircraft could deprive exhausted infantrymen of much needed sleep in the field, or tie up UN nightfighters that could be better employed elsewhere.

Occasionally, the 'Bedcheck Charlies' or 'Lowboys', as GCI controllers called them, would strike it big, validating the communists' commitment to using light aircraft. Such was the case late in the war when a quartet of Yak-18s attacked a fuel dump near Inchon, sending more than five million gallons of fuel up in flames. Flying at low altitude and below the stalling speed of any jet operated by the UN at the time, the 'night hecklers' proved notoriously difficult for the F3D crews to lock up on their radar gear, let alone provide the pilot with enough time to make a firing pass, given the high overtake speeds involved.

Maj Elswin 'Jack' Dunn was the first VMF(N)-513 F3D pilot to encounter a 'Bedcheck Charlie' during a strip alert mission on 26 November. In his command diary recollection of the event, Dunn wrote;

'While in descent at 190 knots for ten seconds, I made a visual on a biplane of the Po-2 type as it passed over a small lake or swampy area. The plane was at "10 o'clock" and slightly below. I immediately turned into the aircraft, which was at 200 ft altitude flying at about 100 knots, and fired at it at the same time, with no results observed. We passed just over him in a left-hand turn. I then went into a port orbit search, but with no success. On returning from this area, a target of opportunity was attacked at YD 2470 – eight trucks. One truck destroyed.'

That same night, six light aircraft – most likely Po-2s – dropped five bombs on Ch'o-do Island but failed to cause any damage. The 'Nightmares' scrambled another strip alert F3D to hunt for the bandit biplanes, and while one RO was able to lock an aircraft up on his radar, the pilot could not establish a workable firing position before overtaking the target and losing contact. North Korea's 'Lowboys' continued to be exceptionally difficult targets for the Skyknight crews throughout the remainder of the war.

The 'Nightmares' finally scored a kill against the 'night hecklers' on 10 December. This kill proved historic in that it marked the first time a jet aircraft fired on another aircraft based entirely on data from its onboard radar systems, with no visual acquisition of the target before firing. Unlike the MiG-15s, which emitted a tell-tale 'glow' from the engine exhaust, the Po-2s and Yak-18s left no such trace, making visual acquisition exceptionally difficult, especially on moonless nights.

In addition to their confirmed kill, 1Lt Joseph Corvi and MSgt Dan George, flying as 'Volleyball 82', fired on another slow-moving target almost immediately afterwards, but did not observe its destruction as with the first one, leading to them only receiving credit for a probable kill. In the December command diary, Corvi recounted;

'At approximately 1915/I [hrs], "Dutchboy" notified all planes in the area that bandits were present. From this time until approximately 1950/I [hrs], continuous vectors and information were given. While on an easterly heading from XD 7040, "Dutchboy" notified "Volleyball 82" that they had overshot a bandit. No contacts had been made up to this time.

'At approximately 1935/I [hrs], the RO picked up a contact at three miles, and since "Dutchboy" had classified the planes in the area as bandits, the lock-on was completed at one-and-a-half miles, with three additional contacts on the [AN/]APS-21 scope. Closed to 1000 yards flying on the [AN/]APG-26 gear exclusively, and commenced firing at that future range. A three-second burst caused the dot to flicker on the [AN/]APG-26 gear as it unlocked and the chase was broken off.

'As I removed my eyes from the scope for visual reconnaissance, three lights were seen as the target passed overhead, with what appeared to be a portion of a wing separated from the main airframe. One light was blue, one a dim white and one a bright white. They seemed to be rotating as the object commenced to fall as if in a spin. It continued to fall and disappeared into the water. A momentary glimpse of the bandit, combined with an estimate of its speed while the tail chase was in progress, leads both myself and my RO to identify it as a Po-2. "Dutchboy" at this time notified "Volleyball" that the trace had disappeared from his scope.

'Almost immediately after this first incident, another vector by "Dutchboy" was received, and a second bandit was picked up at three miles on the [AN/]APS-21 gear, altitude approximately 2500 ft at YD 2060. Closed on the [AN/]APG-26 gear to 1100 yards and commenced firing. Due to the high rate of closure, it was necessary to break off after one burst, and when the break was completed, no visual sighting was made. It is felt that in as much as the [AN/]APG-26 radar was in perfect operating order, and realising the capabilities of this gear, some credence should be given to this incident.'

Although claimed as a Po-2, the ease with which MSgt George was able to lock up two of the hecklers in rapid succession indicates higher radar reflectivity than experienced in confirmed encounters with the wood and fabric Polikarpov biplane, lending credibility to the theory that 'Volleyball 82' had instead engaged metal Yak-18s.

GROUND ATTACK

Lt Col Hutchinson continued his attacks on communist convoys throughout November, culminating in the destruction of three trucks during a rare sortie logged as a night armed reconnaissance and MPQ mission, without any pretence of providing CAP. The MPQ system was a means of controlling air-to-ground missions at night or on cloudy days using a series of radar sites to provide fairly accurate positional data to attack aircraft, culminating with an instruction on when to release their bombs.

On this particular flight, Lt Col Hutchinson made two practice MPQ deliveries working with a controller called 'Anaconda Charlie'. Of note, Hutchinson did not fly with a RO from VMF(N)-513, but with a 'Lt Col Adams' noted as his right-seater on this mission. Although no details are provided, it is likely this was Lt Col (later MGen) Arthur H Adams, commanding officer of F9F Panther-equipped VMF-311 that flew ground attack missions over Korea.

Hutchinson expanded his attempts to involve US Marine Corps Skyknights in the nocturnal interdiction fight in December, flying another night armed reconnaissance mission over North Korea to investigate the airfields at Sinuiju and Uiju for any enemy aircraft on the ground. During this mission, Hutchinson strafed AAA positions and buildings at Sinuiju, all with damage unassessed.

His most lucrative night came on 17 December, when, upon returning from an uneventful NCAP mission, he was directed to attack a convoy moving south on a route known as 'Purple 2'. After multiple passes, and expending 300 rounds of 20 mm ammunition, Hutchinson had destroyed eight trucks. The most unusual of his attacks occurred six days later, when, during another dedicated night armed reconnaissance mission, he expended 200 rounds on a locomotive with ten boxcars, damaging all of them.

While Lt Col Hutchinson conducted the majority of the ground attack missions flown by the F3D, Lt Col Robert Conley and Capt James Weaver also put their Skyknights to work against communist trucks in December 1952. For his part, Weaver ended the month with five trucks destroyed over the course of two missions, including one in which he fired his cannon against both air and ground targets. In his post-mission write-up, Weaver recalled;

'Vectored after bogeys. Got a momentary lock on with [AN/]APG-26 gear, but was unable to fire. Lost contact. Vectored again after bogeys. "Kodak" [Ch'o-do GCI] reported they were nearing Pyongyang. Got visual on an orange airborne light. Received clearance to fire. Expended approximately 60 rounds of 20 mm in a short burst. The light immediately disappeared. Damage unassessed. Requested and received

Although the Skyknight's primary mission was night interception of enemy aircraft, the type's four 20 mm cannon could be devastatingly effective against ground targets. Throughout November and December 1952, VMF(N)-513's CO, Lt Col Homer G Hutchinson, attempted to prove the F3D's air-to-ground prowess against targets of opportunity while returning to Kunsan from missions over North Korea (*Jim Sullivan Collection*)

clearance to strafe trucks near Pyongyang. Expended remaining 740 rounds of 20 mm on trucks at YD 2514 and YD 3020 – four trucks destroyed.'

December 1952 also saw persistent radio communication issues come to a head. Skyknight crews relied on a series of verbal brevity codes to communicate efficiently and effectively with their GCI controllers. Commonly used coded terms included 'Dishpan' to alert others that a crew was off-mission due to a malfunctioning radar, 'Outfield' to notify a pilot he was approaching Chinese airspace, and 'Roger Dee' to confirm that the crew had detected the bogey they were being vectored onto.

This simple system enabled brief but clear communications during intercepts in which multiple nightfighters escorting long bomber streams over North Korea might simultaneously be engaged with different bandits in different areas. To the 'Nightmares" frustration, these communications occurred on radio frequencies not specifically dedicated to NCAP and escort operations. This problem had interfered with the smooth running of B-29 missions from the beginning, and it reached a crescendo in the final weeks of 1952.

Detailing how communications problems hampered his ability to effectively carry out his mission, Capt Oliver Davis wrote;

'Departed K-8 on 19 December 1952 on a prebriefed mission to escort "Sickbat" aircraft 30-45 (B-29s) on their strike in the YD area northeast of Anju. At 2145/I [hrs], a vector was received from "Kodak" on a bandit that evidently was of jet type approaching from the Antung complex. Shortly after this first vector, Blue Channel, which was being used for "Kodak's" control, became so overloaded with conversations from friendly aircraft that the necessary information concerning the enemy's speed, altitude and heading could not be transmitted. Reports by fighter-bombers concerning their activities along the MSRs, reports from light-bombers, and a long transmission by "Abuse" reporting a suspicious flare in his area so completely blocked this channel that control became impossible. In addition, all planes reporting in and out over Point Oboe were using this channel.

'It is my opinion that the overloading of both White and Blue channels at the time I was trying to perform my mission of intercepting an enemy nightfighter, who in turn was attempting to attack our B-29s, prevented me from intercepting and destroying the enemy. The overloading of these channels has been consistently reported by pilots of this squadron who have experienced similar exasperating delays in receiving vital information from GCI controllers. It is imperative that at least one VHF channel be set aside for the use by night interceptors and GCI controllers.'

Davis was not alone in his frustration. Throughout the rest of December, multiple pilots recounted their annoyance with communications delays resulting from excessive third-party radio chatter. In addition to the frustrations of trying to cut through chaotic communications, the 'Nightmares' also dealt with flying so far from 'Kodak' that the GCI controllers could not see bandits approaching either the bomber streams or the F3Ds defending them.

'BAIT' MiGS AND SEARCHLIGHT TRAPS

The communists continued using 'bait-and-trap' tactics in December, with the aim of drawing the Skyknights away from the bomber streams. The ploy involved MiGs flying with navigation lights on, presenting an apparently easy target, but using the type's superior speed to stay just out of the effective range of the F3D's guns while leading them into traps with radar-controlled searchlights that would illuminate the jet for engagement by AAA fire or other MiGs.

Maj David W Thomson was one of the F3D pilots who took the 'bait'. After several fruitless vectors against bandits that out-sped or outmanoeuvred their Skyknight, Thomson and his RO, Lt Schoenberger, received another vector that led them to a bandit with a visible light. Describing the encounter, Thomson recalled;

'A vector of 220 degrees was received and "Kodak" reported we were bracketed by bandits. We were at 30,000 ft when we received this information, and very soon thereafter, I observed a green or blue light, believed to be that of a jet tailpipe. "Kodak" reported another bandit was on our tail, although there was no contact on the tail warning gear. We chased the light while on a westerly heading, and descended from 30,000 ft to 12,000 ft, full power, needle matched, and with our craft shuddering constantly. We were unable to close on the light.

'"Kodak" continued reporting a bandit at a range of eight miles. Visual contact was lost on the light when we were caught by many searchlights all being turned on simultaneously. These lights were definitely radar-controlled and waiting for us, and moderate, inaccurate fire opened up.'

The USAF lost a B-29 on the night of 30 December, apparently due to the bombers arriving over the target area earlier than the time briefed. Lt Col Conley and Capt Oliver Davis – flying as 'Enrage 87' and 'Enrage 88', respectively – both flew as part of the escort package for 'Reliable' flight, arriving near the target area when the raid was already underway. The command diary recorded Davis' perspective as follows;

'While in orbit area at 30,000 ft at 2126 [hrs], "Reliable 24" reported that he was under fighter attack. Turned to a westerly heading and immediately observed an aircraft caught in about ten searchlights at "12 o'clock", 20 miles at 2128 [hrs]. Observed airborne firing on aircraft intermittently for approximately two minutes. Heard "Reliable 24" say he was hit, then observed aircraft on fire at my "11 o'clock" position about 15 miles away. Continued at maximum speed on westerly heading for aircraft that was on fire. Followed around to a southerly heading and continued until fire went out, but did not get closer than ten miles. No radar contact was made on visual sighting.

'At this time, heard "Reliable 26" report that he was under fighter attack. I turned to his area. At 2133 [hrs] observed firing plane at my "10 o'clock" position about 20 miles away while on a northerly heading. Plane firing seemed to expend ammo in about 30 seconds, and plane being fired on caught fire. Closed on burning plane and followed it to approximately YD 5080, then I heard a report [from the aircraft commander] he was bailing out with his crew. At 2140 [hrs] observed plane to crash at YD 5545.

There was at least two minutes between call from "Reliable 26" saying he was bailing out and observation of crash.

'Just prior to hearing "Reliable 26" say he was under attack, heard "Reliable 40" say he was under attack also. Observed some airborne fire at "10 o'clock" while on easterly heading to intercept "Reliable 26".'

Credit for shooting down 'Reliable 26' (44-62011) of the 28th BS/19th BG went to Maj Anatoly Karelin, a MiG-15 pilot from the Soviet 351st IAP. Of the crew of 12, six were listed as killed in action, five survived as PoWs and one died while in captivity. In his analysis of why the Skyknights were unable to protect the B-29s on this mission, Lt Col Conley pointed to three contributing factors: the F3D lacked the speed to catch up to fleeing MiGs; the lack of communication with any GCI station while over the target area; and the inability to establish the positions of the B-29s that were under attack. The lack of communication with GCI stations would continue to hamper Skyknight effectiveness on escort missions over North Korea.

Despite these serious operational problems, VMF(N)-513 recorded the F3D's fourth kill on the night of 12 January 1953 against a MiG-15. Maj Jack Dunn, who flew the mission with RO MSgt Larry Fortin, summarised the incident as follows in the command diary;

'My RO picked up a contact at ten miles that appeared to be heading for the searchlights in the vicinity of YD 0595. "Kodak" called and said the last bomber had departed the target area, but that the bandits were still around. We closed to 4.5 miles and I got a visual on an aircraft that had a white light on each wingtip. The plane was flying north-to-south, about five miles west of Sinanju, at a speed estimated in excess of 500 knots. I was flying at 20,000 ft at the time, the bandits appearing to be about 5000 ft below.

'I immediately called "Kodak" and told them about this plane, and inquired as to whether we had friendly aircraft in the area with running lights on. "Kodak" reported that there were none and investigated further. By this time the aircraft had made a turn, and it headed northeast into the searchlights again. My RO had him on the scope and I had visual. After going directly over the searchlights in pursuit, the bandit turned his lights off and my RO gave me vectors in order to close on him.

'After being well out of the lights, the bandit made a turn back into the searchlights, turning his lights on again. This turn enabled us to close more rapidly on him, and after about five minutes of

Skyknight pilot Maj Jack Dunn (left) and RO MSgt Larry Fortin (right) pose in front of an F3D marked with a red star denoting a kill. Dunn and Fortin were the fourth Skyknight crew to down an enemy aircraft, scoring their victory against a MiG-15 during a B-29 escort mission on the night of 12 January 1953 near Sinuiju, in North Korea. The jet also boasts an impressive mission tally of 49 'nightcap' silhouettes (*Jim Sullivan Collection*)

this figure-of-eight turning, we obtained a lock-on with our [AN/] APG-26 gear.

'It was at this point that I noted the aircraft to be a single engine jet type. I opened fire and let go approximately six bursts. I saw what appeared to be a fire coming from the aircraft. My RO said I had hit him. The flame died out at this point, and I remarked we had apparently missed. The pilot of the bandit began turning his lights off and on at this time. My guns stopped firing, and I charged them again. The bandit made a left turn over the lights and headed northwest.

'He was in a climbing left turn when my RO obtained another lock-on for me, at the same instant I had visual on his lights. I opened fire, and almost immediately he burst into flames. This was at 10,000 ft. He continued his climbing left turn, with the fire increasing. His plane then nosed over and went straight into the deck, exploding on impact.'

That same night, the communists nearly evened the score, with a MiG-15 attacking and scoring hits on a 'Nightmares" F3D crewed by Capt George Kross and MSgt Sell. According to Kross;

'During the retirement phase of a B-29 escort mission on the night of 12 January, at approximately 2350 [hrs] I was momentarily picked up by two searchlights in the Chong'Ju area. Hard evasive turns shook the lights, and a turn toward home base was made. A few seconds later, a firing pass was made on me by an enemy aircraft. Strikes on the airframe, tracers going by and the noise of firing were noticed by my RO, MSgt Sell, and myself. I split-essed from 30,000 ft and commenced downhill rolls. At about 20,000 ft, feeling that we had shaken the bandit, I recovered, and announced to our GCI station that I had a firing pass made upon me.

'The return trip to home base was uneventful. A stall check over the base showed no adverse handing conditions. After landing, a bullet hole in the horizontal fin and a hole in the lower aft fuselage section were discovered. The shell passing through the tail section exploded in the vicinity of the escape chute. The size of the holes indicated 23 mm HEI [high-explosive incendiary] shells had been fired by the bandit. A few minutes after I had been fired on, I heard "Enrage 88", Maj Dunn, announce that he had destroyed a bandit in the same vicinity where I had been hit.'

The 'Nightmares' logged a fifth kill for the F3D on 28 January, with Capt James Weaver and MSgt Robert Becker downing a MiG-15 at low altitude. In the January command diary, Weaver recounted;

'"Kodak" informed me he had a bandit at 20 miles, heading 060 degrees. I started letting down from 30,000 ft, but after two minutes "Kodak" said the bandit had faded from their scope. I orbited and rolled out on a heading of 010 degrees. Several northly vectors were then received from "Kodak", announcing this time I was letting down with needles matched.

'We established radar contact at 30 degrees port, seven miles range, and below. The RO had several other contacts at this time, all port and below also. The range closed to two miles, ten degrees port. Shortly after this, a visual was made at approximately XD 5010, slightly to my port and just below. I was at 1300 ft altitude, with an indicated airspeed of about 500 knots. As I closed in on one jet pipe, it appeared to be a MIG-15.

'I started firing at about 1500 ft and observed two puffs of smoke, at which time the bandit started burning, with flames coming from the centre of the fuselage. The bandit at this time was at 800 ft altitude or lower, still going down, with one wing low. I could not observe his crash as I was unable to turn due to my speed and altitude.'

Unfortunately, the USAF lost another B-29 that night. Multiple accounts in the squadron command diary from pilots who flew escort missions on 27–28 January reference the loss, noting that 'Kodak' had little information on the bandits attacking the bomber (callsign 'Lakeside 27'), and the crew of the stricken Superfortress – 42-27262 of the 370th BS/307th BW – could not provide their own position to enable the Skyknights to assist them.

Poor GCI coverage factored into another B-29 loss on the night of 29–30 January. The 'Nightmares' assigned six Skyknights to escort 'Sonnyboy' flight, with one F3D aborting due to a faulty radar. Several accounts of the mission note that the GCI controllers at 'Kodak' had no information on the bandits attacking 'Sonnyboy' aircraft, despite multiple pilots seeing MiGs make numerous firing passes on the bomber stream. The MiGs finally found their mark on 'Sonnyboy 16' (42-65357 *Shady Lady/Double or Nuthin* of the 28th BS/19th BG), which went down roughly ten miles south of Pyongyang after the entire 14-man crew bailed out, with all of them becoming PoWs – one crewman later died in captivity.

Fortunately – and largely due to the coverage provided by Marine F3Ds – this would prove to be the last combat loss of a B-29 to an enemy MiG-15 in the final six months of the war.

The 'Nightmares' closed out January with the squadron's sixth, and final, kill by an F3D during an escort mission on the 31st. Lt Col Conley and his RO, MSgt James Scott, flying as 'Enrage 87', flew the barrier position as part of a seven-aircraft escort package for a stream of B-29s using the callsign 'Sunbonnet'. After being vectored by 'Kodak' on a bandit that quickly faded out of GCI coverage, Conley warned the escorts closer to the bomber stream to expect company and continued his patrol;

'We started a gentle turn to 090 degrees and radar contact was established at six miles, ten degrees port, and 15 degrees below. A gentle let down was started, 100 per cent power was applied, and we started closing on the contact. The range was close to one-and-three-quarter miles, but a lock-on could not be effected. At this time I saw a plane dead ahead and slightly below, and called "Kodak", reporting that we had a visual on an aircraft that appeared to have his lights on. "Kodak" gave permission to fire.

'At this point the RO also visually picked up the bandit, which was slightly below and flying directly into the moon. We observed the plane was silver in the moon's reflection and had swept wings. The plane had a single jet tailpipe. We closed to less than a half-mile, and when level, and directly behind, opened fire. Two bursts were fired from dead astern, starting at 2400 ft and ceasing at 1000 ft – 250 rounds of 20 mm were expended. Visual contact of the bandit was lost at this time, but the RO reported the bandit was dropping down fast on his scope, and I believe

Operating conditions at Kunsan presented numerous challenges, especially dust and mud. With the Skyknight's low-slung engines being prone to foreign object damage, groundcrews fitted filters over the air intakes for start-up and taxiing to the runway, where they were removed before takeoff (*Jim Sullivan Collection*)

we passed over the top of the bandit. A fast 360-degree turn was made with no radar contact.

'"Kodak" called during the turn and reported they had another bandit, 30 miles south. I rolled out of the turn on a southerly heading to intercept this bandit. This vector was immediately broken off, so we returned to the area where our firing run was made. At this time a ring of fire was observed near the top of a snow-capped mountain. We circled this area and called "Kodak" for a fix, since we believed this was the spot where the bandit had crashed. "Kodak" verified that this was the area where I had opened fire on the bandit.'

Up until February 1953, little had been published in the press about the Skyknight and its role in the Korean conflict. The successes of the preceding months made for a good story, however, and in early February the US Marine Corps publicly released information on the F3D-2 and its victories over North Korea. Whether attributable to publication of information about the F3D (as the command diaries suggest) or simply a result of suffering a rapid succession of MiG losses, the communists sent few MiGs up to challenge the B-29s throughout that month.

MiG activity increased toward the end of February, with the renewed intensity being noted in a mission report from 22 February by Maj David Thomson, pilot of 'Whippet 81';

'At approximately 0440 [hrs], "Parka" (Ch'o-do GCI) vectored "Whippet 81" after a bandit. My RO picked up the bandit at 50 degrees moving from port to starboard. I got a visual on the red and amber running lights and, later, a visual on the tailpipe at four miles, 7000 ft down. The bandit was at an altitude of 23,000 ft, which was approximately the same level as the B-29s. This action occurred within the immediate vicinity of the target, which was at XD 7393.

'We chased the bandit through the bomber stream several times, using 100 per cent power at all times. Only during the turns was it possible for us to close on the enemy. When we had closed to between three-quarters of a mile to one mile, my RO reported that we had a contact on our tail warning gear, crossing from "eight o'clock" to "six o'clock" and closing to within a half-mile. When the bandit stayed on our tail and continued to close, I went into a hard port turn, breaking off the visual on the forward bandit's tailpipe and running lights.

'Just as I entered the "wrapped up" turn [a high-G 360-degree turn], approximately 25 rounds of cannon fire were shot at us by the bandit on our stern. The firing was so close that my RO, hearing the cannons, thought that I was firing my own guns. From the stated above experience, it is this pilot's opinion that the enemy's GCI is excellent.'

Although the 'Nightmares' would not shoot down an enemy aircraft for the rest of the war, they still enjoyed significant success in the escort mission. From February through to July 1953, not a single B-29 succumbed to enemy fire, validating the efficacy of the F3D-2 as an escort. The command chronology for March of that year reflects a change in the enemy's tactics, placing a heavier emphasis on targeting the F3Ds rather than the bombers;

'Instead of sending a host of interceptors to the target area, where they made visual attacks on B-29s locked in the glare of searchlights, he is now sending up jets believed to be equipped with airborne intercept radar in an attempt to better cope with the F3Ds. This is borne out in the fact that his interceptors have been displaying more aggressiveness and have been manoeuvring with the skill that unmistakably indicates they have access to airborne radar, used in conjunction with their excellent GCI control.

'But while these encounters were being pressed between the F3Ds and the MiGs, the B-29s were afforded safe conduct on their raids, which sufficed to ensure success in destroying enemy installations. The combination of our protective escorts and the B-29's bombing skill presents a fighting team that is receiving wide recognition both here and at home. The Bomber Command never ceases to praise its insurance – "The Flying Nightmares".'

Despite the belief that the enemy MiGs possessed on-board radar, little evidence exists to support this claim. Specially-equipped B-29 'Ferret' aircraft, tasked with detecting, recording and identifying the source of enemy radar emissions, found no evidence of airborne radars throughout the Korean conflict. Likewise, modern accounts of Chinese, North Korean and Russian MiG operations based on declassified records give no indication of radar-equipped MiGs being employed by any communist air arm.

The most likely explanation (aside from excellent GCI controllers) is that, as suspected earlier, MiG pilots were able to visually acquire and 'padlock' the bright engine exhausts of the F3Ds, which, by some accounts, could be seen clearly at ranges up to eight miles away. With such an obvious visual signature, MiG pilots needed only to rely on their eyes to stick with evading Skyknights.

In one example of the MiG pilots' newfound aggressiveness, Maj Robert H Mitchell and SSgt Dodd, flying as 'Fruitcake 90', cheated death on the night of 2–3 March while on an NCAP mission north of Ch'o-do. As Mitchell recalled;

'We had just been directed to a target supposedly three miles dead ahead of us at 150 degrees. We were in the XE 2427 area at the time. We received no contact. I reported this to "Parka" and they told me to commence a port orbit, as they had lost the bandit. "Parka" had previously warned us that there were two bandits in the area, so, rather than making a continuous orbit, I was stopping every 40 degrees or so to give the RO a chance to look for targets on both nose and tail gear.

'We had just stopped on a heading of about 090 degrees when I noticed a couple of reddish fireballs ahead of me and slightly below. I had previously noticed what I believed to be light AAA fire on the ground, and thought that this was some of it, so I started a sharp turn to the left. Then I heard cannon fire [assumed to be from an enemy aircraft because of the fairly slow cyclic rate] for several seconds, and noticed red balls going over the port wing. I jammed the stick forward, cut off all power, popped full dive brakes and got out of there. During the dive, the aircraft felt as though it was out of control. I thought I had gone through the Mach, but the ASI was on 300 knots, and the initial attack started at 20,000 ft.

'Dodd, the RO, also saw the red balls going over the left wing and over the aircraft. He saw a considerable number of red balls in front of the aircraft. I started pulling out of the dive at around 14,000 ft and the aircraft was shaking violently, so I eased up and we came out at 11,000 ft. I pulled in the dive brakes, and the aircraft was still shaking badly, and we had little elevator or rudder control though the speed was now down to 200 knots.

'When the enemy aircraft made the firing pass at us, I had thought that I heard a noise of metal tearing, in addition to the cannon sound, so I assumed that we were hit. I headed for open water, about 15 miles away, on a heading of about 20 degrees, and called "Parka" to inform them. "Parka" gave us a steer for their station, stood by with facilities and alerted air-sea rescue.

'I had gradually added full throttle, and the aircraft kept on shuddering for about two minutes and the airspeed did not increase above 210 knots. I still had little rudder and aileron control. Gradually, the shuddering diminished, and the aircraft started picking up speed. I informed "Parka" that I thought we would make it home.'

The perception that the enemy flew radar-equipped MiGs persisted with encounters like that experienced by Maj Thomson and his RO, 1Lt Schoenbarger, on the night of 12 March;

'Immediately upon arriving over the target, we picked up two tail contacts which rapidly closed on us. Evasive action lost these contacts momentarily. Retained altitude of 27,000 ft during this evasive action. At that time I saw first bombs go off on target and approximately 20 searchlights came on, focusing on a spot about a half-mile north of us. We immediately picked up another tail contact, with another three contacts coming in within a matter of seconds. It is impossible to give any detail from here on out, for during the next 15 minutes we had a total of six attacks made on us. We saw, heard and felt a long burst that was fired at us.

'For a period of approximately ten minutes we constantly had at least one tail contact while taking hard and desperate evasive action. We went through the target area from 30,000 to 5000 ft during those ten minutes, diving vertically usually in a wrap-up turn and with the aircraft buffeting most of the time at its limiting Mach. We would do the hardest evasive action, including vertical dives, only to spot the bandits four or five miles to the rear of us.

'Pilot can only assume that; 1. At least 12 bandits were well positioned prior to bombers' attack; and 2. It was technically impossible for GCI to acquire visual contact to enable bandits (or bandit leader) to follow us. Only an experienced pilot using airborne intercept gear in an aircraft with superior performance to ours could have maintained the persistency of the chase.'

The use of single MiGs as 'bait' continued to be the preferred tactic employed by communist pilots. The latter could either lure a solitary F3D into a searchlight and AAA trap, or use the MiG-15's superior speed under the guidance of highly-proficient GCI controllers to remain tantalisingly just out of range, while leading a pursuing Skyknight into an ambush by several MiGs emerging from low-altitude. While the MiG-15 held speed and manoeuvrability advantages over the Skyknight, as well as enjoying better and more proximate GCI coverage, the F3D held several strengths that levelled the playing field.

Foremost among the F3D's advantages was the AN/APS-28 tail warning radar. From the very first contacts with MiGs in October 1952 through to the end of the war, the VMF(N)-513 command diaries feature dozens of accounts each month from aircrew citing the tail gear as the reason they evaded successful engagement by the enemy, despite the communists' clear superiority in speed, manoeuvrability and GCI coverage. The March 1952 command diary provides perhaps the strongest praise for the AN/APS-28;

'This one piece of equipment, or a similar one designed for the same purpose, is considered a mandatory requirement for any all-weather fighter, especially since the jet tailpipe can be seen from such a long distance at night.'

The same summary included a description of the tactics the 'Nightmares' used to evade tail contacts;

'Various manoeuvres have been used by pilots of this squadron in order to break away from a visual contact obtained by an enemy fighter on their jet tailpipes. When a bandit has been picked up on the tail warning gear and has been radar observed long enough to foresee his intentions, it becomes mandatory to execute a manoeuvre to break his visual. On one occasion, a pilot of this organisation executed a loop, others have split-essed, and still others have executed a rapid level reversal of course. All of these have proven successful up until the present time.'

The 'Nightmares' received some welcome assistance in March 1953, as the USAF finally permitted its F-94B Starfire nightfighters to operate over North Korea. From the last week of March through to the end of the war, F-94s joined the F3Ds in the escort role, serving largely as barrier CAPs between the bomber streams and the MiG bases north of the Yalu.

NON-GROUND ATTACK MISSIONS

The official US Marine Corps history of the Korean conflict, a five-volume series titled *US Marine Operations in Korea*, states that Skyknights from VMF(N)-513 employed general-purpose bombs on air-to-ground sorties during the battle for the Nevada Cities complex – a series of hilltop outposts along the lines between UN and communist forces – on 27 March 1953.

However, the squadron's command diary for that month makes no mention of any F3Ds conducting ground attack missions on the 27th, but it does include several F7Fs flying ground attack sorties.

Furthermore, where the official US Marine Corps history records additional air-to-ground sorties by F3Ds on 10 April, for that specific date, the command diary only notes the 'Nightmares' committing Tigercats to ground attack missions. The likelihood is that the official history erroneously attributed the close air support (CAS) missions flown by VMF(N)-513's F7F crews to the F3D.

Although the communists had altered their tactics to increasingly target the Skyknights, direct attacks on bomber streams also continued. On the night of 19 April, Capt Lengel (who, along with his RO, 1Lt Long, was a USAF F-94 exchange crewman from the 319th Fighter Interceptor Squadron) witnessed three firing passes against the B-29s he was escorting. Maj Patton and SSgt Rothblatt also saw two of these firing passes from 'Grease Cup 84' and pursued two bandits as they egressed at high speed, quickly opening the distance and fading from Rothblatt's scope – a common occurrence, given the MiG's speed advantage.

The 'Nightmares'' continued success in preventing B-29 shootdowns throughout the spring of 1953 brought high praise from FEAF Bomber Command. As noted in the official US Marine Corps history of the Korean War;

'In an April 1953 message from Air Force Col Harvey C Dorney, commanding officer of the 19th BG, to Lt Col Conley, Dorney wrote "19th BG Airborne Commander and crews participating in attack on Sinanju Bridge Complex, 11 April, have high praise for nightfighter protection. All feel that without their protection, severe damage or loss of B-29s would have resulted".'

Further praise for VMF(N)-513's escort was noted in a Pacific Fleet Evaluation Report, which noted;

'The enthusiasm with which this Marine aid to the Air Force has been received by FEAF Bomber Command indicates that VMF(N)-513 had successfully adapted its equipment and personnel to a mission usually associated with Air Force operations, making an important contribution to inter-service cooperation, but even more important, to tactical progress in the night escort of bomber formations.'

Although the 'Nightmares' had not scored a kill since January, the upside was that the MiGs had not either, although it was not for lack of trying. Communist fighter pilots remained as aggressive as ever, relentlessly going after Skyknights and Starfires, as well as continuing to target B-29s. VMF(N)-513 ROs were just as likely to pick up a MiG on their tail warning gear as they were on their nose gear, with the majority of the contacts going undetected by Ch'o-do GCI.

The communists clearly enjoyed superior GCI, even if their radar equipment was not quite as good as that used by UN forces. The close proximity of the Chinese GCI sites to the areas targeted by FEAF's B-29s resulted in a far clearer radar picture for the communist 'scope' operators than that available to their American counterparts much further south who were trying to track dynamic air battles at the extreme edge of the range of their equipment.

The 'Nightmares' suffered their fourth F3D loss (the third occurring on 16 May 1953 with a landing mishap, which injured then-commanding officer Lt Col Ross Mickey) on 30 May 1953 when Capt James Brown and RO Sgt James 'Red' Harrell failed to return from a B-29 escort. Flying F3D-2 BuNo 127024 under the callsign 'Grease Cup 25', Brown's final transmission was not a distress call, but a request for approach assistance into Kunsan as he was returning to base. Although a Chinese MiG-15 pilot claimed to have shot down a jet nightfighter on the night of 29 May, the recovery of Sgt Harrell's remains from the mud flats near Kunsan in July 2001 confirm this claim to be fraudulent.

Between May and early June, VMF(N)-513 relocated from K-8 airfield to K-6, further north along the west coast of South Korea near Pyongtaek. The move included a shift of control from Marine Air Group (MAG) 33 to MAG-12, and was made gradually to allow the 'Nightmares' to continue meeting operational commitments without interruption. The move north enabled slightly more time on station for F3Ds operating over North Korea.

Sparse MiG contacts on escort missions characterised the second half of June, with most crews reporting 'Negative vectors, contacts, or intercepts' on nearly every mission during that period. If a contact was detected, it usually departed the area quickly and faded from the pursuing Skyknight's scope.

The Naval Aviators and ROs of VC-4 Det 44N 'Nightcappers'. Standing, from left to right, are Lt(jg) Bob Bick, Lt G G O'Rourke, VC-4 CO Cdr Joe Gardiner, original detachment OIC Lt Cdr Howard Terry and Lts Bobbie Allen and Glen Wegener. In the front row, again from left to right, are CPO Linton Smith and POs Ben Latawiec, Howard O'Neil, Pete Karnincik and David Lockwood. This photograph was taken at NAS Atlantic City, in New Jersey, in early 1953 whilst Det 44N worked up for its deployment aboard *Lake Champlain*. Terry and O'Neil were killed in a mishap shortly after taking off from NAS Atlantic City at night in poor weather on 18 March 1953, Cdr Gardiner concluding the cause to be a thrown compressor blade (*Paul Bless Collection*)

'NIGHTCAPPERS' JOIN THE FIGHT

On 10 June 1953, USS *Lake Champlain* (CVA-39) arrived off the east coast of Korea with four F3D-2s and five aircrew from Navy Composite Squadron (VC) Four, Detachment 44N, among the ship's embarked Carrier Air Group (CVG) 4. Nicknamed the 'Nightcappers', VC-4 also embarked F2H-2 Banshees and F4U-5Ns. Aboard *Lake Champlain*, the F3D proved a curiosity for other aircrews, and a nuisance for deck handlers. Some Naval Aviators chastised the F3D crews for flying such a large warplane that did not carry any bombs and had no viable daylight mission.

Lake Champlain's deckcrew, unaccustomed to aircraft as large as the F3D, damaged Skyknights while moving them from the hangar deck to the catapults on more than one occasion. The slight downward cant of the engine exhausts heated the metal deck plates to such high temperatures prior to each catapult shot that deck crews had to wait for the plates to cool before moving the next aircraft into launch position. The ship's wooden deck fared little better, as even at idle the heat from the F3D's engines occasionally ignited the petroleum products which had leaked into the wood from countless aircraft!

Of greatest concern to the Skyknight crews was the ship's H-8 hydraulic catapult system, which had to be used at near-maximum power to get an F3D off the deck with enough speed to continue forward flight. Twice during *Lake Champlain*'s 1953 cruise, the wire catapult bridle connecting the Skyknight to the catapult shuttle disengaged just as the catapult fired, sending the shuttle – at full power without the resistance of a 27,000-lb aircraft to mitigate its speed – crashing into the stops at the forward end of the deck, causing severe damage and taking that catapult out of commission until it could be repaired.

To the deckcrews and command staff aboard *Lake Champlain*, the Skyknight was a massive, deck-burning, (*text continues on page 43*)

A VC-4 Det 44N F3D-2 prepares to catch an arrestor wire during carrier qualification training on board USS *Franklin D. Roosevelt* (CV-42) in June 1952, prior to the detachment's Korean War deployment. As with the rest of the units assigned to CVG-4, VC-4 Det 44N had to have all of its crews flightdeck qualified before *Lake Champlain* headed out on its first, and only, combat cruise on 26 April 1953 (*National Naval Aviation Museum*)

COLOUR PLATES

1
F3D-1 BuNo 123767 of VMF(N)-542, MCAS El Toro, California, 1951

2
F3D-2 BuNo 127026 (also possibly 127020) of VMF(N)-513, K-8 (Kunsan), South Korea, 1953

3
F3D-2 BuNo unknown of VMF(N)-513, K-8 (Kunsan), South Korea, April 1953

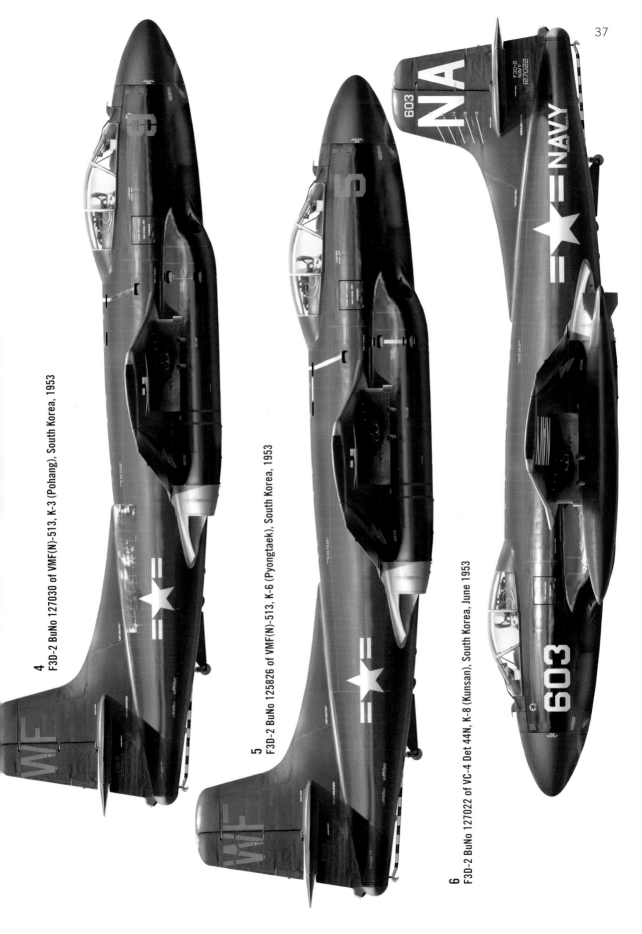

4
F3D-2 BuNo 127030 of VMF(N)-513, K-3 (Pohang), South Korea, 1953

5
F3D-2 BuNo 125826 of VMF(N)-513, K-6 (Pyongtaek), South Korea, 1953

6
F3D-2 BuNo 127022 of VC-4 Det 44N, K-8 (Kunsan), South Korea, June 1953

7
F3D-2 BuNo 127027 of VMF(N)-513, K-3 (Pohang), South Korea, 1954

8
F3D-2Q BuNo 125850 of VMCJ-3, MCAS Iwakuni, Japan, 1958

9
F3D-2Q BuNo 124596 of VMCJ-3, MCAS Iwakuni, Japan, 1958

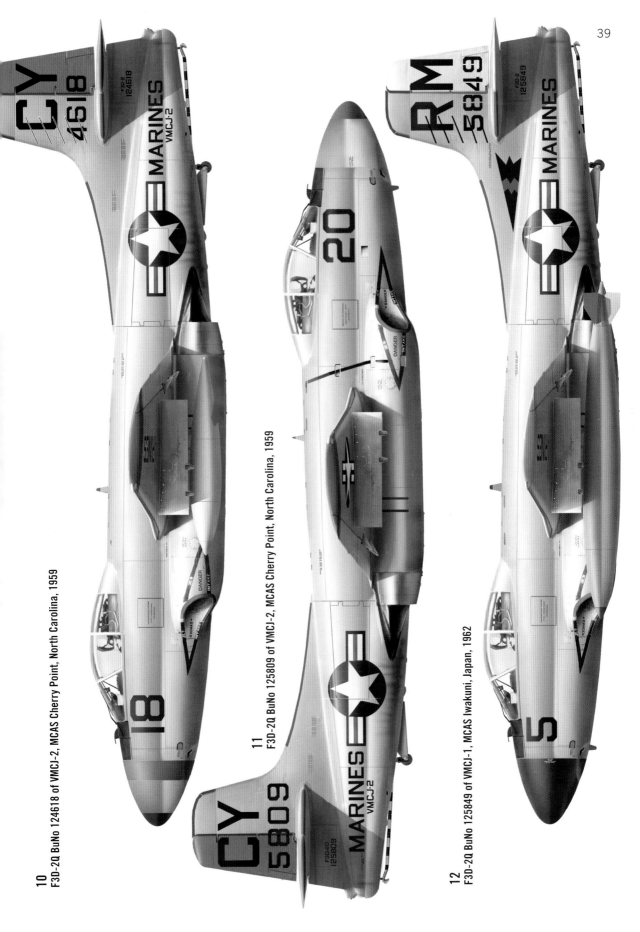

10
F3D-2Q BuNo 124618 of VMCJ-2, MCAS Cherry Point, North Carolina, 1959

11
F3D-2Q BuNo 125809 of VMCJ-2, MCAS Cherry Point, North Carolina, 1959

12
F3D-2Q BuNo 125849 of VMCJ-1, MCAS Iwakuni, Japan, 1962

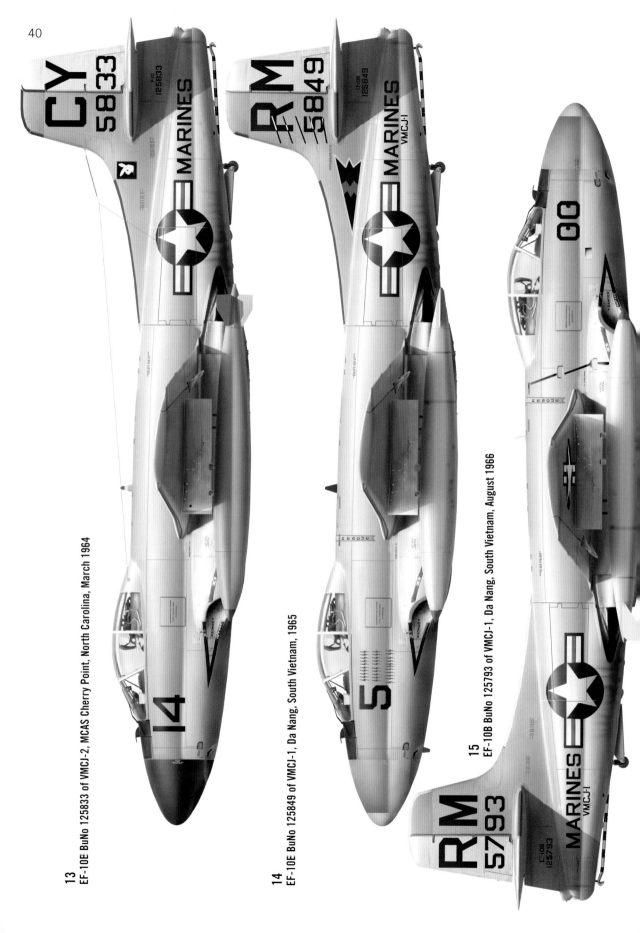

13
EF-10E BuNo 125833 of VMCJ-2, MCAS Cherry Point, North Carolina, March 1964

14
EF-10E BuNo 125849 of VMCJ-1, Da Nang, South Vietnam, 1965

15
EF-10B BuNo 125793 of VMCJ-1, Da Nang, South Vietnam, August 1966

16
EF-10B BuNo 127051 of VMCJ-1, Da Nang, South Vietnam, August 1966

17
EF-10B BuNo 127051 of VMCJ-2, MCAS Cherry Point, North Carolina, May 1967

18
EF-10B BuNo 124632 of VMCJ-1, Da Nang, South Vietnam, September 1967

19
EF-10B BuNo 125869 of VMCJ-1, Da Nang, South Vietnam, October 1967

20
EF-10B BuNo 124620 of VMCJ-1, Da Nang, South Vietnam, May 1968

21
EF-10B BuNo 124619 of VMCJ-1, NAS North Island, California, February 1969

Prior to deploying to Korea, VC-4's Skyknight crews trained extensively on night intercepts and radar-based dogfighting from their home base of NAS Atlantic City. Many of the unit's Naval Aviators and ROs were also cross-trained as GCI controllers. BuNo 127022 was photographed on a training flight during the early weeks of the *Lake Champlain* deployment, the jet having been marked with the 600-series modex applied specifically to Det 44N aircraft when embarked with CVG-4 (*Tailhook Association*)

catapult-breaking nuisance that did not carry any bombs and could not contribute on daylight missions. The pilots and ROs of Det 44N felt every ounce of their contempt.

To add to these frustrations, when *Lake Champlain* arrived in-theatre, Skyknight aircrews struggled to get flying hours at night just to maintain proficiency, let alone be launched on any actual nocturnal missions. When detachment Officer-in-Charge (OIC) Lt Jerry O'Rourke pleaded with CVG-4's carrier air group (CAG) commander, Cdr J R Sweeney, for night hours, he was met with suggestions that the Skyknights strap on bombs for daylight attack missions. CAG even used the ship's nightly movie showings as an excuse to not launch them after sunset.

Desperate to get his crews into the fight, and to prove their mettle on the type's first combat cruise, O'Rourke relented and allowed the Skyknights to be worked into daylight missions. In his memoir *Night Fighters Over Korea*, he recalled;

'We substituted for other planes on day carrier patrols. We struggled in orbits overhead in bright sunlight, watching Banshees and Sabres climb high above us with ease. We ran escort for photo-planes but couldn't keep up with them, even when they slowed and we used max power. We ran a day road recce – about the silliest mission in the world for a huge, radar-loaded "Whale" [the name used by Skyknight crews to refer to the aircraft], since our only armament was quadruple 20 mm guns.'

After several fruitless days of watching other aircraft launch on missions they were designed for, while the Skyknight crews filled in for tasks the F3D was ill-suited to, O'Rourke petitioned to go ashore to join up with VMF(N)-513 at Pyongtaek. Eager to get rid of the plate-melting, deck-burning, catapult-breaking, no-bomb-carrying, movie-night-ruining Skyknights, CAG Sweeney finally relented, and on 19 June the four F3Ds of Det 44N launched from *Lake Champlain*'s deck and headed for their new home among the Marines at K-6.

In contrast to the chilly détente with which they co-existed with others aboard *Lake Champlain*, the 'Nightcappers' arrived at K-6 to Marines greeting them with warmth and enthusiasm. As O'Rourke recalled;

'It was like coming home to mother at Christmas time. They were happy to see us. Our four shiny airplanes augmented their resources. Our crews, even with their limited experience, looked good to them, and the prospect of having some 45 additional mechs and technicians was manna from heaven for their hard-pressed ground maintenance gang.'

Thankful for the help, VMF(N)-513 quickly worked the 'Nightcappers' into the flight schedules. O'Rourke noted;

'After an initial checkout mission with a Marine RO, we Navy types were fully integrated into the squadron. We were scheduled just like any other teams. Our airplanes intermingled with the Marine planes, even though we tried to do most of the flying in them ourselves.'

For as thoroughly as O'Rourke and the other US Navy crews trained in clear, concise intercept communications prior to deploying, operational security concerns necessitated a bit of ambiguity when it came to communicating with controllers at Ch'o-do;

'Our own controllers, down in their lonely vigil on distant Ch'o-do, would give us vectors, or courses to fly. Instead of repeating these orders very carefully, in the most clear and concise manner, as we had been taught in training, we would grunt a quick reply, then proceed to fly our own vector, which might be somewhere near, but never on, the course ordered by Ch'o-do. To do otherwise was folly. If MiGs were coming after us, any prior knowledge concerning headings, speeds and altitudes was highly valuable to them, so why give it away for free?'

A crew from Det 44N possibly scored the Skyknight's final kill of the war. Lt(jg) Bob Bick was the det's youngest pilot, who, despite his youth and relative inexperience, had been hand-picked for the detachment for his skill and aggressiveness as a Naval Aviator and his willingness to volunteer for any mission. Further, at the squadron's home base in Atlantic City, on nights he was not scheduled to fly, he volunteered as a GCI controller,

The US Navy contributed four F3D-2s and five combat crews to the Korean War, and three of those aircraft are visible in this view of *Lake Champlain* at anchor off Aden on 18 May 1953. Unwieldy to operate aboard ship and unable to be worked effectively into night operations, the Skyknights found a home ashore with VMF(N)-513 for much of *Lake Champlain*'s time on station with Task Force 77 off Korea. Note the F4U-4 Corsairs on the bow and the AD-4 Skyraiders on the stern, aligned for steerage assistance (*US Navy*)

After the Armistice went into effect, the aircrews and maintainers from VC-4 Det 44N returned home to NAS Atlantic City, but they left their aircraft behind at Pyongtaek for VMF(N)-513. BuNo 127030 was a former 'Nightcappers' jet, retaining the US Navy's Glossy Sea Blue paint scheme. Note the Det's insignia peering out from behind the '9' modex on the nose of the aircraft. This jet later served with VMF(AW)-542 (*Paul Bless Collection*)

learning both sides of the nightfighter business as thoroughly as he could. Bob Bick arrived at K-6 with one goal – to bag a MiG.

He finally got his chance on 2 July 1953. While flying a routine NCAP mission with CPO Linton Smith, Bick radioed Ch'o-do to report a contact on his radar. The controller, who struggled to follow Bick on his scope, detected no bogeys, so was of little help when the Naval Aviator requested authorisation to fire shortly after reporting the contact. Before the controller could get a handle on the situation, Bick radioed that he had fired on a bandit and had set it on fire – a transmission quickly followed by another announcing he had taken several hits from a 37 mm cannon. Shortly thereafter, Bick and Smith's Skyknight disappeared from the controller's scope.

O'Rourke speculated that Bick – who, along with Smith, had only been flying missions for less than two weeks – fell for the 'bait' tactics communist pilots had been using for months, focusing on the 'bait' MiG while multiple others jockeyed for position on his tail. Two nights later, a VMF(N)-513 F3D crewed by Capt Lote Thistlewaite and SSgt William H Westbrook failed to return from an NCAP in the same area where Bick and Smith were last heard from. This proved to be the final Skyknight casualty of the Korean conflict, bringing total F3D losses to six – five US Marine Corps and one US Navy – in exchange for six confirmed kills (one of them contested by Soviet records), one probable (Corvi's second 'Night Heckler') and Bick's flaming MiG-15.

US Marine Corps and US Navy Skyknights closed out the war providing CAS for UN forces during a fierce battle between 19 and 26 July. Several key outposts, including two dubbed 'Berlin' and 'East Berlin', sat along what was certain to become the dividing line between a post-war North and South Korea as armistice talks progressed. Both sides fought for strategically-advantageous positions along what was assured to be the post-war Demilitarized Zone (DMZ). While claims of F3Ds providing CAS earlier in the war were likely misattributions of sorties flown by F7F Tigercats, at the time of the battle for the 'Berlin' outposts, VMF(N)-513 had fully transitioned to the Skyknight, leaving no ambiguity about which aircraft the 'Nightmares' brought to the ground fight that final week of the war.

At 2200 hrs on 27 July 1953, the 1st Marine Aircraft Wing Post-Armistice Plan went into effect, committing US Marine Corps aircraft and crews to armistice enforcement operations over South Korea. In addition to defending South Korea from communist aerial attack from the north, Skyknights from VMF(N)-513 also enforced a No-Fly Line south of the DMZ designed to keep a buffer of neutral airspace between the two Koreas. In concert with USAF fighters from Fifth Air Force, the 'Nightmares' protected this boundary from incursion from the south as well as from the north.

Another provision of the Armistice restricted aerial ports of entry into South Korea to five airfields, of which K-6 at Pyongtaek was not one. As such, VMF(N)-513 F3D-2s going to or coming back from Japan (such flights were usually maintenance-related) had to pass through K-9 Pusan East or K-2 Taegu.

VMF (N)-513 remained in Korea after the Armistice, flying border enforcement missions through 1955. During this period, it marked BuNo 127027 with a '12^{7}/$_{8}$' modex, subscribing to the superstition that '13' is an unlucky number. This aircraft also wore a red star beneath its cockpit at one point, although the unit's command diaries fail to indicate which crews scored specific kills in it (*Tailhook Association*)

A pair of F3D-2s from VMF(N)-513 high over South Korea in 1955. Although the war had ended two years prior, the 'Flying Nightmares' remained in-country to undertake border enforcement missions (*Tailhook Association*)

CHAPTER TWO

COLD WAR ELINT

In 1958, VMCJ-3 deployed to MCAS Iwakuni, where the squadron began flying ELINT missions known as 'Shark Fins' off the coasts of China, North Korea and the Soviet far east as part of PARPRO. BuNo 125850 was an early participant in these operations, serving with VMCJ-3 from 1958 through to 1965, when it was transferred to VMCJ-2 (*Tailhook Association*)

lthough obsolete as a fighter only two years after the Korean War had ended, the F3D-2 held promise as a replacement for the electronic warfare (EW) variant of the AD-5 Skyraider equipping Marine Composite (VMC) squadrons at the time. The Skyknight offered three distinct advantages. First, the cavernous fuselage and large radome could be repurposed for the receivers and transmitters needed for the EW mission. Second, the wide side-by-side cockpit seating arrangement could easily accommodate a pilot and an electronic countermeasures officer (ECMO). And third, the US Navy and US Marine Corps were retiring the bulk of their Skyknight fleets in favour of faster radar-equipped fighters, freeing up enough aircraft to equip three VMC squadrons (soon to become Marine Composite Reconnaissance or VMCJ squadrons, which flew both EW and photo-reconnaissance aircraft).

The VMC community initiated the development of what would become the F3D-2Q (EF-10B from 1962 onward), the EW variant of the Skyknight. In early 1955, VMC-3 at MCAS El Toro selected F3D-2 BuNo 124620 as the first to be modified for the EW mission, this process being led by veteran ECMOs WO Joe Bauher and MSgt E R 'Doc' Grimes.

The F3D-2Q's EW kit included an APR-13 Panoramic Surveillance Receiver (later replaced by the ALR-8), an APA-69A direction-finder and an ALA-3 pulse analyser. This receiver suite covered most radar frequencies used by Soviet-built air defence systems. For jamming, the

F3D-2Q employed a pair of 200-watt ALT-2 noise jammers mounted in the Skyknight's spacious nose. Noise jamming creates electronic 'noise' that degrades a radar operator's ability to discern an 'echo' return of the signal generated by his emitter from the noise created by the jammer.

The two prototypes engaged in a series of tests designed to validate the EW fit at Naval Ordnance Test Station China Lake, in California, and the White Sands Missile Range, in New Mexico, with the systems being refined after each one. With the Bureau of Aeronautics approving a formal engineering change and funding for conversion of 35 F3D-2s to F3D-2Qs, VMCJ-3 took delivery of the first production example in December 1956. By the end of 1958, VMCJ-1, -2 and -3 had completed the transition from AD-5N to F3D-2Q.

The first deployment for US Marine Corps F3D-2Qs occurred in July 1958, when VMCJ-3 was sent from El Toro to MCAS Iwakuni, in Japan. The squadron's primary role was to provide EW threat simulation for air defence and naval forces in the western Pacific, but commanding officer Lt Col Robert R Read quickly secured another mission for VMCJ-3's Skyknights.

The Peacetime Aerial Reconnaissance Program (PARPRO) employed USAF and US Navy aircraft to conduct peripheral photographic and electronic reconnaissance of communist bloc nations from international or friendly airspace. Most aircraft types involved in PARPRO missions were bombers or maritime patrol types modified for electronic reconnaissance. With its sensitive electronic receivers, the F3D-2Q proved a useful tool in collecting intelligence on radar systems in China, North Korea and the Soviet far east. Beginning in September 1958, VMCJ-3 flew PARPRO missions under the codename 'Shark Fin'.

Between December 1956 and December 1958, the US Marine Corps converted 35 F3D-2s from nightfighters into dedicated EW aircraft designated F3D-2Qs to replace its ageing Douglas AD-5Q Skyraiders. VMCJ-3 took delivery of the first F3D-2Q in December 1956. Two of the jets seen in this photograph were written off in accidents, with BuNo 125806 becoming the first Skyknight lost in the Vietnam War when it crashed into the sea off Da Nang on 31 July 1965, and BuNo 127060 being damaged beyond repair on 1 July 1969 (*Tailhook Association*)

Given the distances involved, the 'Shark Fin' missions demanded greater endurance, and VMCJ-3 began outfitting its Skyknights with 300-gallon drop tanks under each wing, versus the 150-gallon tanks that F3Ds had flown with during the Korean War. For missions up toward Vladivostok, in the Soviet Union, Skyknight crews staged out of Misawa air base in northern Japan. While flying from here enabled VMCJ-3 to collect electronic intelligence (ELINT) along the far eastern reaches of the Soviet Union, operating out of northern Japan provided significant challenges. Capt Chuck Houseman, a Skyknight pilot who did an Iwakuni tour with VMCJ-1 in 1964–65, recalled some of the problems posed by the weather at Misawa;

'If you've ever been to northern Japan in the wintertime, it's like the south in the summer. A thunderstorm in the south crops up and is violent as hell for about 30 minutes to an hour, then it dissipates and it's blue sky again. It's that way in Misawa, where it would snow at the rate of a bad thunderstorm. It was so thick and heavy that you were lucky to be able to see ten feet in front of you. It was almost like a thick fog.

'Then, of course, the next thing was getting home. Hopefully, there was the option to return home and land at Misawa, because if they had one of those damn snow showers, we would be lucky to find the base, much less the runway. That's why they had those running lights alongside the runway that were at least three feet in the air and lit up. When you came in either during, or after, one of those snow showers, you kind of plopped into the snow and you had to shut the engine down before there was a

This aerial view of the VMCJ-1 flightline at MCAS Iwakuni was taken in 1961. Six F3D-2Qs can be seen, along with F8U-1P Crusaders, also from VMCJ-1, and A4D-2 Skyhawks from a forward-deployed US Marine Corps attack squadron (*MCARA*)

wall of snow. It was always good to be on the ground in Misawa, because you had no alternative, and it was mighty cold out there if you had to step out of that thing.'

Other forward operating locations for 'Shark Fin' missions included Osan, in South Korea, and Tainan, in Taiwan.

During the late 1950s the Soviets started moving toward a missile-centred approach to air defence, developing the SA-2 surface-to-air missile (SAM) to defend military targets and population centres throughout the Soviet Union from American long-range bombers. During a 1959–60 deployment to Iwakuni, VMCJ-1 was the first to locate a 'Spoon Rest' early warning radar near Vladivostok. Then-Capt Jim Doyle, an ECMO on that deployment, recalled;

'That first time I was out there in 1959–60, we detected, recorded and reported the first "Spoon Rest" radar out of Vladivostok. That was a prime signal for us. One of our guys, MSgt Bo Boyett, detected the signature, and it was right there around 965 megahertz, which was the same frequency range as our TACANs out there, so there's was a very difficult frequency range to work. But Boyett got a good recording of it, got a couple of cuts, and myself and a guy by the name of "Woody" Woods analysed the tapes, ran it through the tape recorder and ran it through an audio machine, measuring the pulse width on it versus other signals. That's how we identified it as a "Spoon Rest", versus another signal, sent it up to [the Pacific Command ELINT centre at] Fuchu, and they came back and said, "Oh yeah, that's a 'Spoon Rest'".'

THREATS AND INTERCEPTS

Although crews flying PARPRO missions remained in international airspace and relied on standoff receivers to collect intelligence, communist air arms from the nations being spied on routinely sent MiGs up to intercept and investigate the surveillance flights. In most cases, these intercepts involved MiGs harmlessly flying wing on an F3D-2Q before turning back. Recalling one such peaceful intercept, Chuck Houseman said;

'The first time we were intercepted, they reported that we were taking pictures of them, as we were carrying 35 mm hand-held cameras. Normally, it would be on the pilot's side where the interceptors were, and the ECMO would lean across and snap some pictures of them. And the Russians would report, "They're taking pictures of us. What should we do?" One of the Russian controllers had a sense of humour and said "Smile". Who would have thought the Russians had any sense of humour at all?'

As amicable as intercepts with Soviet MiG pilots could be, pilots from other communist nations in the region were decidedly humourless. In his book *Top Secret*, ECMO J T 'Jerry' O'Brien wrote;

'One didn't wave at the Chinese or North Koreans. In fact, we went to some length to avoid contact with the Koreans and the Chinese. On flights from Taiwan, we were usually covered by a flight of Chinese Nationalist F-86s.'

On 16 June 1959, NKPAF MiG-17s attacked a US Navy P4M-1Q Mercator flying an electronic reconnaissance mission 50 miles off the east coast of Korea. While its crew managed to recover safely in Japan, despite the aircraft being heavily damaged (it was later declared a write off) and the tail gunner being wounded, the attack – which occurred while US Marine Corps Skyknight crews were flying similar missions – drove home the serious turns these flights could take. Although the VMCJ aircrews managed to avoid such unpleasantness, one particular PARPRO mission drew fire of another sort from an unexpected source – the US National Security Agency (NSA).

In late January 1965, VMCJ-1 marked a single EF-10B with some interesting graffiti that raised eyebrows both in the USSR and at home. Chuck Houseman, who flew the marked-up aircraft on a 'Shark Fin' toward Vladivostok, recalled;

'This was not authorised, but we thought we'd jazz up the situation a little bit, so we somehow or another were able to come up with the Russian language that said 'JOIN THE U.S. MARINE CORPS' and painted it on the side of the fuel tanks on the F-10s [the F3D-2Q had been redesignated the EF-10B in September 1962]. There was a conversation, we learned later on, when the interceptors came up – they got a little closer than usual and were reading it off to the ground controller. They reported it, and there was no response, so they reported it again and there was still no response, so they dropped it.

'The painting on the fuel tanks caused some big turmoil in the background in Washington, D.C., with the NSA wondering what the hell was going on. By the time the information rolled down to us, the second flight was up there with those same markings, and they didn't want to turn him around when he was already on his way out, but they passed the word down, "Paint that damned thing over and get rid of it".'

Judicious flying helped prevent MiG encounters, with pilots denying intercepts by beginning their turns back toward Japan before the relatively

Following the completion of VMCJ-3's 1958–59 deployment to Iwakuni, VMCJ-1 relocated there from Hawaii to continue flying 'Shark Fin' missions. Over the six years that followed, VMCJ-1 was manned on a rotational basis by Marines from VMCJ-2 at MCAS Cherry Point and VMCJ-3 at MCAS El Toro. BuNo 127041 transferred to VMCJ-1 from VMCJ-3 in the early 1960s, and it subsequently had the unfortunate distinction of being the only Skyknight to have definitely been downed by the enemy. On 18 March 1966 the jet was hit by an SA-2 fired by the 61st Battalion of the 236th Missile Regiment, causing it to crash minutes later (*Tailhook Association*)

short-legged MiGs could close the distance on them. As EF-10B pilot then-Capt Art Bloomer recalled from his 1961–62 tour with VMCJ-1;

'I flew a lot of the "Shark Fin" missions out of Misawa, where we headed straight out towards Vladivostok, getting to within 20 miles of it. I never did get intercepted, as I was always turned before then, and we'd have MiGs on our tail. They followed us for 50–60 miles out to sea when we were headed back to Misawa, then they would break off and go somewhere else.'

In addition to MiGs, Skyknight crews faced another threat on the 'Shark Fin' missions – 'spoofer' beacons, which were deceptive navigational aids intended to lure aircraft conducting PARPRO missions into communist airspace, where they could be engaged by ground-based air defences. Art Bloomer (who retired as a Brigadier General) encountered 'spoofer' beacons on multiple occasions;

'I saw two "spoofers". One was in China, trying to lure you over the mainland, and the other one was around Seoul, trying to lure you into North Korea. It was the same frequency, but it was more powerful. You had to make sure you were right on the frequency, or you could easily get locked onto the wrong ADF [automatic direction finder]. It was a low-frequency approach beacon – one of those fixes that enable you to make a self-contained approach without radar.'

Despite these threats, the US Marine Corps never lost a Skyknight to MiGs or air defences on a 'Shark Fin' mission.

As well as providing valuable data on Soviet-designed radar systems, the PARPRO mission helped VMCJ units develop skills that would prove to be of critical importance during the Vietnam War. The Skyknight's EW suite, while useful, lacked a built-in geolocation capability. It could help ECMOs and analysts identify what type of emitter the receivers were detecting, but could not provide data on where that emitter was located. Without the ability to report on an emitter's location, the best analysts

In addition to 'Shark Fin' missions, EF-10s in Japan provided ECM aggressor training for US and Japanese air, land and naval forces, giving them opportunities to train in a radar-degraded environment. Such training frequently involved 'Whales' creating chaff corridors with ALE-2 pods, like the pair seen here under the wings of BuNo 125810 in an image from VMCJ-1's 1963–64 Iwakuni rotation cruise book. This particular aircraft later became a 'Super Whale' (*MCARA*) could discern from mission recordings was that the crew had encountered a certain radar at some point, with little else in the way of useful data. An ECMO named TSgt Roy 'Moose' Simolin devised a solution to this problem that he dubbed the 'Hack system'.

In his book *Top Secret*, Jerry O'Brien, a contemporary of Simolin's, described the 'Hack system';

'Shortly after a takeoff, the ECMO would turn on his tape and record an announcement identifying the flight number, et cetera. Then, once within range of the enemy radar, he would begin to search for a specific radar frequency. If he found the radar emitting, he would turn on the tape, record the exact time and begin his work identifying the radar by using the word "Hack" as the main lobe came by. In the operator's earphones, a radar PRF [pulse repetition frequency] would sound as a buzz as the various lobes passed the aircraft at a specific tone. There might be two or three radars present, all of them with similar tonal qualities. Thus, using this "Hack system", the operator could differentiate between signals. It was primitive, but it worked.

'The word "Hack" would hopefully identify the specific radar that he was working, versus several other similar signals that might be present. He would usually add a bearing, such as "Hack, 320 degrees", or "Hack 1.2", thus giving the width of the pulse. Back on the ground, he would analyse the tape and obtain exact frequencies, pulse widths, pulse repetition rates, scan rates and the bearing to the radar. Then he would resolve the navigation, as best he could, and submit a report of the flight.

'When Roy first devised his signal identification system, there were a lot of people who didn't care for it. Of course they had never tried it and didn't understand it, but they still didn't like it. Eventually, after "Moose" proved that it would work, the Army, Navy and Air Force all adopted the procedure.'

The 'Hack system' helped not only with emitter location, but with specific data on the signals being intercepted. As Art Bloomer recalled;

'I flew with "Moose" many times. He was able to find eight beams on a "Bar Lock" [a Soviet early-warning radar] that we had intercepted, and he was trying to collect information on it. He was the first guy to find out that the "Bar Lock" had eight beams on it by using the "Hack system".

CUBAN PARPRO

The success of the 'Shark Fin' missions in Asia paved the way for similar operations, dubbed 'Smoke Rings', flown around the periphery of newly-communist Cuba, a mere 90 miles from Key West, Florida. In mid-1960, crews from VMCJ-2 routinely flew navigational training sorties to the US Navy base at Guantanamo Bay, on the southeastern end of Cuba.

ECMOs who had done an Iwakuni tour with VMCJ-1 or VMCJ-3 and flew 'Shark Fins' suggested adding ELINT collection to these flights, both to provide real-world training in detecting, locating and analysing recordings of Soviet-built emitters, and to monitor any expansion of Soviet air defence systems in Cuba, given the growing ties between the nation's communist leader Fidel Castro and Moscow.

establishment of multiple SA-2 sites indicated that the communists were up to something worth defending.

Given the SA-2 threat in Cuba, in mid-October CINCLANT authorised Operation *Blue Moon* – a series of low-level photo-reconnaissance missions flown primarily by US Navy RF-8As from VFP-62, with assistance from VMCJ-2's RF-8s and USAF RF-101 Voodoos. Concurrent with the *Blue Moon* missions that began on 23 October, VMCJ-2 continued to undertake ELINT flights around the periphery of Cuba to determine the location of air defence systems.

On 14 October 1962, imagery from a U-2 overflight revealed what the Soviets had erected the SA-2 sites to defend – nuclear-capable SS-4 MRBMs. Another flight two days later discovered more SS-4s, as well as longer-ranged SS-5 IRBMs. Placement of these missiles in Cuba meant the Soviets could strike nearly anywhere in the continental USA with far less warning than with intercontinental ballistic missiles launched from within the USSR. So began the '13 days' of the Cuban Missile Crisis.

As tensions escalated, US Marine Corps 'Whales' stood ready to provide jamming of 'Fire Can' and 'Whiff' AAA radars in Cuba, but crews remained concerned about the 'Fan Song' radars used to guide SA-2s to their targets, for there was little known about the system. Responding to pressure from Castro to defend the island from air attack, local Soviet SAM commanders escalated the crisis significantly on 27 October when they gave the order to fire on a USAF U-2 without authorisation from Moscow, bringing the aircraft down and killing its pilot, Maj Rudolph Anderson. Khrushchev relented the next day, agreeing to withdraw the IRBMs and MRBMs from Cuba.

The US Marine Corps continued to fly ELINT missions around Cuba for the rest of the decade until VMCJ-2 retired its EF-10Bs – as much to keep tabs on Castro's air defences as to expose new ECMOs to Soviet-built emitters before they deployed to Vietnam.

As with the 'Shark Fins', these flights carried the risk of interception by Cuban MiGs. Due to the ranges involved in these sorties, communication

VMCJ-2 provided both EF-10Bs for electronic reconnaissance of Cuban air defences and RF-8As to fly Operation *Blue Moon* photo-reconnaissance sorties with VFP-63 during the Cuban Missile Crisis (*Tailhook Association*)

between 'Whale' crews and their controllers often got spotty, resulting in occasional unintended penetrations of Cuban airspace, luckily with no hostile response. To remedy this, VMCJ-2 outfitted several EF-10Bs with an additional high-frequency (HF) radio, enabling controllers to warn crews at longer ranges. Aircraft so equipped carried a wire antenna running from just behind the cockpit to the top of the tail, with another wire connecting to the fuselage on the left side of the aircraft.

Despite this fix, incursions still occurred, typically the result of winds aloft and cloud cover obscuring the Cuba coastline, giving pilots no visual reference. This was the case in 1967 when 1Lt Terry Whalen was an ECMO on such a flight;

'Some guys you liked flying with, some you didn't, but there was one guy, his name was Ariel Cross. I got to know him pretty well. He was a quiet guy and I'm a smart aleck, and I was always trying to get him to lighten up a little bit. We used to fly down to NAS Key West and fly around Cuba to piss Castro off. It was good training.

'I was flying down there with Ariel one day, and he kind of drifted into Cuban airspace. Supposedly, they scrambled a couple of jets to see what was going on, and the Navy scrambled a couple of jets to see what we were doing. Nothing happened, but it could have been a bad incident, I suppose. We got back, and I thought it was funny, but Ariel, being such a serious guy, he was really angry at himself. I kept joking about getting to go to Cuba and drink their booze, and all that stuff, but he wasn't having any of it.'

In Asia, VMCJ-1 continued flying 'Shark Fins' through the spring of 1965, when the proliferation of Soviet-made air defence systems (including the SA-2) in North Vietnam resulted in a request for US Marine Corps EF-10Bs to provide jamming escort during missions as part of Operation *Rolling Thunder* – President Lyndon B Johnson's air campaign against North Vietnam's communist government.

Skyknights from VMCJ-2 flew the Cuban ELINT missions – known as 'Smoke Rings' – from NAS Key West. Given the distances involved when undertaking sorties to the farthest reaches of southern Cuba, pilots occasionally lost radio contact with their controllers at Key West, who could not warn them they were penetrating Cuban airspace. To avoid the potentially lethal fallout from such incursions, VMCJ-2 added a long-range HF radio to some of its EF-10Bs, with a wire antenna trailing from the rear of the cockpit to the tip of the tail, as seen here on BuNo 127051 (*Tailhook Association*)

warning radars, and the ALT-19, which could jam 'Fire Can', 'Whiff' and 'Fan Song' fire control radars, 'Rock Cake'/'Stone Cake' height-finding radars and – most importantly for these early missions – the 'Spoon Rest' radars used for GCI control of the MiGs.

On the 29 April mission, the Skyknights departed Da Nang at ten-minute intervals, with their jammers on continuously once they crossed the DMZ, dropping chaff to confound the radar picture for the enemy controllers in advance of the strike package arriving over the target. ECMOs switched off the jammers only once they had crossed the DMZ again en route to Da Nang.

Within a month of arriving at in-theatre, VMCJ-1's Skyknights were in such high demand by both the USAF and the US Navy that they were flown at a rate that outpaced the maintenance and supply systems' ability to support them. In his comments on a draft of the official US Marine Corps history of the Vietnam War, Lt Col Corman remarked;

'During May and June the EF-10Bs were operated at 300 per cent of normal utilisation. Due to the limited total of EF-10B resources (both aircraft and spare parts), Brig Gen [Keith B] McCutcheon [1st Marine Air Wing (MAW) Commanding General] directed the utilisation rate be limited to 200 per cent or 60 hours per month per plane. To achieve this, a 1st MAW liaison officer was assigned to US Military Assistance Command, Vietnam's electronic warfare coordinating authority, and VMCJ-1 was tasked to support Air Force and Navy operations in only high threat areas; i.e. strikes inside the SA-2 missile envelope complex.'

This achieved the desired reduction, but the resultant 200 per cent utilisation rate over peacetime usage continued to push maintainers and the supply system to their limits.

From its earliest missions in Vietnam, the limitations of the EF-10B were abundantly clear. The ECM tasking demanded that Skyknights be on station prior to the arrival of the strike aircraft, and then be the last to leave once all strikers had dropped their bombs. Missions as far north as Hanoi and Haiphong required the use of external drop tanks to provide both the range and time on station needed, and even then, 'Whale' crews flying what was known as the 'western track' egressing North Vietnam into Laos often diverted to Ubon, in Thailand, for fuel, before continuing home to Da Nang.

Whether carrying 300-gallon fuel tanks, jamming pods, chaff pods, or combinations thereof, the already-sluggish 'Whale' became a chore to get off the ground in the heat and humidity at Da Nang. Chuck Houseman recalled;

'We were so loaded down that on that 10,000-ft runway, ordinarily we'd be airborne at 5000 ft under normal conditions at sea level, but I swear to God, when we were going on those deep missions north of Hanoi especially, we damned near used the entire 10,000 ft. You would see the end of the runway rushing up at you, but you kept the faith and pulled it off properly, and hopefully everything worked. That's where big, thick, wings came in handy, because even though the "Whale" was slow, the wings provided good lift and got us airborne.'

While most pilots and ECMOs who flew it primarily referred to the EF-10B as the 'Whale' or 'Willie', the type's seeming reluctance to leave the

EF-10B aircrew from VMCJ-1's initial detachment at Da Nang. Standing, from left to right, are 1Lt L J Kuester, Capts Chuck Houseman and L A Marshall, 1Lt Jerry Westphal, SSgt D A Krimminger, CWO2s C V Cooke and E H Beresford, Lt Col Otis Corman and CWO2 Vern Small. Kneeling, from left to right, are 1Lt C W Thompson, Capt J T Pycior, Sgt R H Kreckman, Capt H I Bond and 1Lt W R Simons (*Warren Thompson Collection*)

ground at Da Nang earned it another, less frequently-used nickname – the 'DRUT', or 'turd' spelled backwards.

'WHALE' PILOTS AND ECMOS

To understand VMCJ-1 during the Vietnam War, some discussion of how EF-10 pilots and ECMOs were trained is necessary. For as important an asset as the EF-10B was, it was almost as if the aircraft had been forgotten about by the naval aviation community at large.

No formal training programmes existed for either pilots or ECMOs assigned to fly Skyknights. Pilots in VMCJ squadrons typically arrived via the pipeline for another type operated by the squadron – the RF-8A Crusader, RF-4B Phantom II or EA-6A 'Electric Intruder' – and they were then cross-trained on the EF-10B. As 'Whale' pilot Dave Foss recalled;

'There was no manual, there was no NATOPS [Naval Air Training and Operating Procedures Standardization] programme and there was no RAG [Replacement Air Group] to go through for training. When I was at Cherry Point one day, somebody said "Hey, you haven't flown the F-10 yet, go fly it". I said, "Okay, where's the manual?" He said, "You have an F3D manual that's Korean War vintage", and it was basically not even applicable to the airplane. It was basically flown on rumours that circulated – things like don't fly faster than 300 knots indicated airspeed, and the minimum altitude if you had a problem to escape from the airplane is 2000 ft, straight and level in controlled flight.'

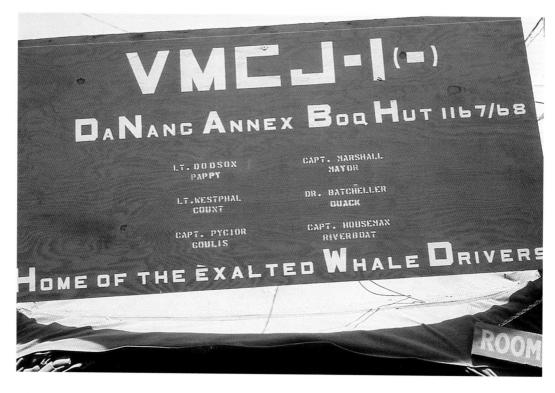

New ECMOs transitioning to the 'Whale' fared little better. 1Lt Hugh Tom Carter graduated from Naval Flight Officer (NFO) school at Pensacola in 1967 and expected assignment as an F-4 Radar Intercept Officer (RIO). Instead, he – like many others – received orders to VMCJ-2 at MCAS Cherry Point, in North Carolina, assigned as an ECMO in the EF-10B. Carter recalled;

'So everybody that showed up in that timeframe routed down through MAG-14 to VMCJ-2 in 1967. That's when John Suhy, myself, Terry Whalen, Herman Shipman – all of us – showed up. When we got there, there was no Mather Field [the USAF's dedicated aerial navigation training base in California], no school for EW down in Pensacola. It was all on-the-job training taught by "Moose" Simolin, Meek Kiker, Joe Stone and Rush Morgan – we called him [Morgan] "The Coach" because that's how we kind of felt, like we were on a team and he was the coach. He taught us all this stuff, mostly about the systems on the aircraft, but we weren't getting a lot of theory. We got a little bit of that in NFO school in Pensacola, but not much.'

Only a handful of new EF-10 ECMOs received formal EW training when Dave Colegrove, Almart 'Al' Olsen and Charles 'Dean' Percival went through the USAF's Electronic Warfare Officer (EWO) school at Mather AFB in 1967.

The veteran ECMOs were Marines who entered the VMCJ community as senior non-commissioned officers or warrant officers in the 1950s, with some either going through formal commissioning programmes or accepting temporary commissions in 1962 when the US Navy mandated that aircrew on tactical jets be commissioned officers. Some – like GySgt Hank 'Robbie' Robinson (who kept his enlisted rank while flying with

Accommodation at Da Nang consisted of several general-purpose tents that did little to keep the dust and noise out. Note the 'VMCJ-1(-)' designation, which denoted that the unit was a composite reconnaissance squadron. VMCJ-1 operated EF-10Bs for EW and RF-8A Crusaders for photo-reconnaissance. Only the Skyknights deployed to Da Nang initially, while a detachment of VMCJ-1 RF-8As, and their pilots, augmented Crusader-equipped VFP-63 Det D on board USS *Coral Sea* (CVA-43) while the carrier was undertaking combat operations from *Yankee Station* in 1965 (*Warren Thompson Collection*)

VMCJ-1) and MSgt Fred Killebrew – were World War 2 veterans well into their 40s while flying in Vietnam.

Robinson had been a US Army paratrooper fighting in France and the Netherlands, and he proudly wore the French *Croix du Guerre* and Dutch *Order of Wilhelmina* on his dress uniform, while Killebrew had been a tail gunner on SBD Dauntless dive-bombers in the Pacific. 1Lt Louis White was another World War 2 veteran, having received the German Iron Cross for shooting down a Soviet fighter while serving as a young Czechoslovakian Flak gunner – a decoration Headquarters Marine Corps denied White authorisation to wear on his dress uniform.

These 'old hand' ECMOs brought more than a decade's worth of EW experience with them to Vietnam, and they were critical to the success VMCJ-1 enjoyed in protecting friendly strike aircraft from North Vietnamese air defences.

FIRST LOSS, FIRST SAM SITE STRIKE

Despite increasing amounts of AAA fire over North Vietnam in July 1965, VMCJ-1's EF-10Bs consistently returned to Da Nang without so much as a scratch until 31 July. That night, during an ECM mission, 1Lt Milton K McNulty and CWO Vernard J Small crashed into the Gulf of Tonkin in EF-10B BuNo 125806. There was no distress call and no survivors. The jet was over the water when it was lost, so it is unlikely the Skyknight's demise could be blamed on enemy action.

One week earlier, a new and deadly chapter in the Vietnam War had commenced. Although US forces had evidence showing that SA-2 sites had been in North Vietnam since early April 1965, up until this point in the war, no SAMs had been fired at American aircraft. With US intelligence indicating the North Vietnamese were receiving assistance from Soviet technical advisors in establishing these sites, they remained on the Pentagon's restricted target list for fear of killing a Russian advisor and risking a Cuba-like crisis with the USSR.

Shortly after VMCJ-1 arrived at Da Nang, an F-105D of the 18th Tactical Fighter Wing, flying from Korat Royal Thai Air Force Base, made a precautionary landing at the airfield. The aircraft was duly parked on the squadron's ramp, and after a few days without any crew showing up to claim the Thunderchief, the Marines painted their 'Romeo Mike' code on the tail and the squadron's markings on the fuselage (*Tailhook Association*)

On 24 July Capts Roscoe Fobair and Richard Keirn were part of a four-ship of F-4Cs from the USAF's 47th Tactical Fighter Squadron/ 15th Tactical Fighter Wing out of Ubon air base, in Thailand, escorting an F-105 strike when one of three SA-2s fired from a site 40 miles west of Hanoi hit their Phantom II, making them the first US airmen to be downed by a SAM.

The loss drove home the importance of the jamming being provided by EF-10s and EB-66s, which had both been flying escort missions since late April. Wanting to punish the North Vietnamese SAM operators and degrade the communists' ability to employ these deadly weapons against American aircrews, Adm Ulysses S Grant Sharp, Commander-in-Chief of US Pacific Command, authorised simultaneous strikes against two known SA-2 sites west of Hanoi on 27 July. All six of VMCJ-1's EF-10Bs took part in this historic mission, dubbed *Spring High*, which involved 48 Thailand-based F-105s attacking two SAM sites.

Capt 'Duke' Steinken, a veteran of the US Marine Corps EW community going back to the Korean War, was a RIO with F-4B Phantom II-equipped VMFA-542 at this time, the unit having arrived at Da Nang just prior to VMCJ-1. With the latter squadron lacking sufficient ECMOs to man all six 'Whales' committed to the 27 July mission, Lt Col Corman requested two RIOs with EF-10 experience from MAG-11 F-4 squadrons. In a recollection of the mission penned for the Marine Corps Aerial Reconnaissance Association, Steinken wrote;

'For some reason or another VMCJ-1 did not have enough ECMOs to fly the six-plane mission that was fragged by the USAF. I was a RIO with VMFA-542 at that time, but had previously been an EWO/ECMO with VMC and VMCJ squadrons for eight years and held an EW secondary MOS [Military Occupational Speciality]. [CWO-2 William E] "Dink" Riley, another former ECMO then with VMFA-513, and I were requested to fly the max-go EF-10B mission. I asked my CO if I could fly the mission, and he said, "Go ahead, have fun!"'

'I was teamed with Maj [Jerry] Mitchell, the VMCJ-1 Operations officer, but at the scheduled launch time our aircraft [BuNo 125849] did not have all the ECM equipment installed. The other five aircraft had to depart without us to meet their IP [Initial Point] times. About 15 minutes later, the VMCJ-1 CO came by and said they were going to cancel our mission, but Maj Mitchell said, "No Skipper, we are ready to go", and we immediately taxied out and took off for North Vietnam.

'We had been briefed to fly over water to the Haiphong area, then west to our IP near the SAM sites outside of Hanoi, where we would set up a racetrack pattern at 20,000 ft. We were about 110 miles from Da Nang over water abeam Vinh when I calculated we were not going to make our IP on time on the briefed course. I plotted a new direct course, and we transitioned over land towards Hanoi. As we passed to the west of Thanh Hoa, I intercepted numerous "Fire Can" fire control radars and commenced jamming them, breaking their radar lock-ons.

'Maj Mitchell said "'Duke', look out here", and I saw the entire area was black with heavy AAA bursts. We got through that and arrived at our IP right on time as the F-105s began to attack the SAM sites in intervals

Just as VMF(N)-513 used 'nightcap' symbols to denote missions in the Korean War, VMCJ-1 stencilled a red lightning bolt onto its 'Whales' upon the completion of an ECM mission over North Vietnam. On 17 July 1965, Maj J J Mitchell and ECMO Capt 'Duke' Steinken flew jamming support for the first USAF strike against known SAM sites in this aircraft – BuNo 125849. Although the USAF lost six F-105s on this raid, none fell to radar-guided AAA or SAMs (*Tailhook Association*)

for more than 20 minutes. Collectively, the six EF-10Bs intercepted and jammed GCI, fire control and SA-2 "Fan Song" target-tracking radars, and we also dispensed chaff. The "Fan Song" radars indicated active SAM sites, and threat warnings to the strike force were given, although no missiles were reported during the attack while we were on station. MiG formations were reported passing through the area during the attack, but there were no engagements.

'After the attack was over, we did not attempt to join the other EF-10Bs as we departed alone and headed for the coast and feet wet. About 33 miles north-northwest of Vinh, we received a MiG alert at our "six" at 14 miles. We had two 20 mm guns, but when we had crossed into North Vietnam and test-fired them, the port weapon immediately jammed. The starboard gun fired about five shells and it jammed, so we had no guns [a common occurrence]! We descended very rapidly to a low altitude over water and proceeded to Da Nang, where we were the first EF-10B to land. We learned later that the USAF had lost several aircraft, but none to radar-controlled AAA or SAMs.'

Losses on this mission totalled six F-105s. The operation had demonstrated the dangers of flying at low-level over the heavily defended areas around Hanoi and Haiphong, where even AAA with jammed guidance radars could be aimed visually.

FUEL MANAGEMENT

Whether supporting USAF raids in the Hanoi area or US Navy strikes near Haiphong, *Rolling Thunder* missions pushed EF-10Bs to the limits of the type's range. Unlike the aircraft being supported, the EF-10 lacked an aerial refuelling capability. Furthermore, the unique needs of certain missions demanded that each Skyknight carry an ALE-2 chaff dispenser under the left wing and/or an ALQ-31 jamming pod under the right wing. Moreover, the tactics of the time required EF-10s to be on-station before the strike packages arrived, and to remain on-station until the last element of a strike was out of range of enemy air defences.

Precise planning to minimise transit time and time on station, while still providing the required support, was critical to the success of each mission, but sometimes even that was not enough. Describing one method of ensuring the EF-10 had enough station time to provide jamming support through the full duration of these strikes, Chuck Houseman told the author;

'We had to conserve fuel because we were so loaded down with these electronic jamming pods. In order to carry them, we had to leave off at least one of the 300-gallon fuel tanks and, in some cases, both. That would give us at least a 30, if not 40, per cent reduction in time on target or time in the air. As a result, on the way to the Hanoi area, it took us a while to get up there. However, if we could take off early enough and pretty much cruise to the target area, we could shut an engine down in order to save gas.

'When we got up there and on station, we lit off the other engine and did the job. After that we were very low on fuel to get back, so as soon as we got out of what was allegedly a threat area, we would shut an engine down again and pretty much cruise home. We were always very, very low on fuel. But it was paramount that we accomplish the mission, so we had to take all kinds of shortcuts, and safety be damned. We wanted to do the job the best way we knew how to.'

Although careful fuel management enabled Skyknight crews to provide the required jamming support on these long-range missions, being the last aircraft out of the threat area left the EF-10s vulnerable to attack by North Vietnamese MiGs. Despite carrying a pair of 20 mm cannon (more for ballast than for self-defence according to crews), 'Whale' pilots like Houseman knew they were sitting ducks should any MiGs pursue them;

'When it was over, we had stirred up a bees' nest of course, and they knew what our capabilities were and what we were doing, and I'm sure one of their priorities was to get us. They would launch when the Air Force was headed back to Thailand and the Navy was heading for the carriers. That left us there with our ass hanging out, looking for a good thunderstorm, which were usually west of Vietnam.

Four EF-10Bs taxi out from VMCJ-1's ramp at Da Nang for an active ECM mission over North Vietnam. To the left of the quartet is a USAF F-102A Delta Dagger, and on final approach is an F-4B from VMFA-542 – the US Marine Corps' original Skyknight unit. The two 'Whales' in the foreground carry ALQ-31 jamming pods under their right wings. The ALQ-31 could carry two jammers, typically either the ALT-17 for early warning radars like the 'Knife Rest B', or the ALT-19, which jammed most fire control radars like the 'Whiff', 'Fire Can' and even the 'Fan Song' (*Tailhook Association*)

'We'd have to go over into another country in order to fly through the cloud coverage, and only with great reluctance and for a brief period of time would we shut an engine down when you were in that kind of condition because you could stall at the other end, and then you were in deep shit. That was the challenging part of the mission, operating in an old bird, unarmed and with no escort.

'One of the carriers [USS *Oriskany* (CVA-34)] had a Marine Crusader squadron on it that was conducting strikes under the Navy "helmet", and we got word to 'em and said, "Look, if you've got any extra gas when you've finished your strike and we're out there helping you, can you hold hands with us for a while on the way back to Da Nang before you dash over to your carrier?" They said "Oh hell yeah, we thought you guys had some kind of escort". So we called Saigon and told them to kick the damned politics out of the way and give us what we were due. They did.

'They would come up and fly wing on us for a while, at least down to Vinh just north of the DMZ, then they'd peel off and go to their carrier. That was VMF(AW)-212. I knew some of the guys because it was a small world in Marine Corps aviation. Sooner or later, you knew damned near everybody.'

VMCJ-1 officially received fighter escort in August 1965 when the Commanding General of 1st MAW ordered F-4s from MAG-11 to protect the EF-10s. Having flown with VMCJ-1 as an ECMO during the SAM site strike on 27 July, Capt 'Duke' Steinken flew another historic mission, this time in the back seat of an F-4B from VMFA-542 in August. As he explained;

'The Commanding General of 1st MAW ordered fighter escort for all the EF-10B missions over North Vietnam. The first escort mission flown in August 1965 was kind of an historical moment for the Marine Corps, as we were to be the first Marine fighters to enter communist territory since the last war. The first escorts consisted of two F-4Bs, one flown by the CO of VMFA-513 and the other by the CO of VMFA-542, allowing both units to share in the glory on this historic flight. Since I was teamed with the CO of VMFA-542, I made this mission as well.'

Although primarily an EW platform, the EF-10B also carried a K-17 reconnaissance camera in an unpressurised port at the rear of the aircraft.

Being first in and last out of target areas over North Vietnam, EF-10Bs were often left to fend for themselves as they egressed hostile airspace. To ensure the 'Whales' had the protection they needed, Brig Gen Keith B McCutcheon, Commanding General of 1st MAW, ordered the US Marine Corps F-4B squadrons at Da Nang – VMFA-513 and VMFA-542 – to escort EF-10Bs on missions over North Vietnam. Here, a VMFA-542 Phantom II can be seen in the background as BuNo 125793 taxis by at Da Nang. This aircraft was the last EF-10B lost by VMCJ-1 in-theatre, the 'Whale' failing to return from an ECM mission near the DMZ on 17 July 1968 (*Jim Sullivan Collection*)

Chuck Houseman led the first unofficial photo mission (hardly any were official) for the EF-10 in Vietnam, leading a two-ship formation over Haiphong harbour on what proved to be a fruitful, if ill-advised, endeavour;

'We always wanted to help anybody we could, and a couple of our eager intelligence people said, "Boy, wouldn't it be nice if we could come up with some photos of the activity in Haiphong?" They wouldn't let the Air Force or the Navy fly over that activity, where they were unloading all the ships with the missiles and whatnot. And so – unofficially – we thought we would repay and obtain a favour or two to our, shall we say, spook contacts, and we took some pictures, but we damned near lost the ballgame there. They were really "loaded for bear", and we didn't have any way to counter that particular heavy stuff that was coming our way.

'We provided some very good photos. What they did with them, who used them, we never saw. But we repaid a favour and hopefully provided a service to someone who could make good use of it.'

Although rarely used, the camera in the EF-10B was occasionally employed by crews throughout the type's service in Vietnam, typically on a one-off basis. For example, Maj Jim Doyle photographed a North Vietnamese patrol boat off the coast of Vinh in early 1966 as a target of opportunity, 1Lts Gail Sublett and Wayne Whitten captured a 'Cross Slot' radar north of the DMZ in August 1966 and Maj Art Bloomer and his ECMO 'Moose' Simolin photographed a search radar in Laos in 1968.

SAM HUNTING

Having failed to do any appreciable damage to the SAM sites attacked on 27 July 1965, the USAF made further attempts to destroy SA-2 batteries throughout August, with VMCJ-1 providing jamming support for all three missions that month. The squadron command chronology documents these operations, conducted on 9, 11, and 31 August, as follows;

'The strikes on the 9th and the 11th were unsuccessful due to the sites having been vacated during the interim between site location (by a combination of tactical ELINT and photo-reconnaissance) and strike execution. VMCJ-1 participation on these two missions involved a passive/active ECM role consisting of missile radar detection, strike aircraft warning and then electronic jamming of the emitter.

'The SA-2 site strike on the 31st was considered a success from an EW point of view in that the site was located purely by tactical ELINT (the missile radar having been stimulated into emitting by other reconnaissance and tactical aircraft penetrating the general area), with the strike force having been launched within a short subsequent time interval (in this case, about two hours). The missile site was visually located by the strike force but only one strafing run was accomplished. VMCJ-1 participation on this mission was limited to launching on the strike phase from a ground alert status and conducting electronic jamming against the missile radar under attack.'

The failure of these strikes confirmed that the USAF's tactics simply were not what the SAM-killing mission demanded. After the 31 August strike, the USAF and US Navy temporarily backed away from targeting

SAM sites. Subsequently, VMCJ-1 worked with the USAF in developing the tactics and validating the systems used for 'Wild Weasel' anti-SAM operations. Jim Doyle flew several of these missions as an ECMO;

'Initially when the Air Force was trying to come up with a hunter-killer airplane – the "Wild Weasel" – we did some work with some F-100s. We also had a F-105 one time that came up. We would meet him over Laos at a pre-determined time, then we would take a run-in from Laos into North Vietnam towards Vinh, where the AAA had the "Fire Cans" and different kinds of radars. They would lock onto something and tell us what they had, and we would confirm, saying "Yeah, I got that too", or "No, no, no".'

One of the more interesting missions VMCJ-1 flew in the August–September timeframe involved escorting a flight of US Navy Douglas A-3 Skywarriors on a bombing raid, during which rather anachronistic tactics were employed. Chuck Houseman, who flew one of the two EF-10s providing jamming support on this mission, recalled;

'I will never forget that, because the Navy had the big brother to our F3D called an A3D. It was a larger "Whale", and they loaded them up with bombs and wanted them to knock out a rail junction at Vinh. When they flew over, it reminded me of World War 2, with the B-17s dropping bombs on some damned city in Germany. We were monitoring and supporting them very close by, and there was a little bit of AAA activity going on, but these guys just flew straight and level over the target and counted down, then "bombs away", and I said "My God, this is not World War 2". They were flying flat and level and probably pretty damned slow in order to drop those bombs from the fuselage, and they got away lucky. That was only one time, and they missed the damned railway junction completely.'

OCTOBER CADRE/NOVEMBER *IRON HAND*

Prior to deploying to Vietnam, VMCJ-1 had been manned on a rotational basis, with a cadre formed from both stateside VMCJ squadrons (-2 at Cherry Point and -3 at El Toro) and training at El Toro prior to deploying to Japan. The initial group of pilots, ECMOs and maintainers that deployed to Vietnam did so halfway through their one-year western Pacific deployment. In early October, an advance echelon arrived at Da Nang to prepare for the arrival of the replacement cadre.

Jim Doyle, a veteran ECMO with 'Shark Fin' experience, arrived as part of this advance echelon and flew his first mission, with Capt Mike Gering, supporting a US Navy strike against targets near Hanoi on 8 October. By the end of the month, the rest of the squadron had arrived to replace the Marines that had served at Da Nang since April. The newly arrived crews jumped right into combat missions, including one of the earliest US Navy attempts to destroy a SAM site.

In the wake of the failed July SAM site strike by the USAF, the US Navy began developing its own approach to the suppression of enemy air defences (SEAD) mission, which it called *Iron Hand*. The second successful *Iron Hand* mission occurred on 7 November (the first had taken place on 17 October), with VMCJ-1 providing crucial jamming support for a strike against several SA-2 sites from the 236th Missile Regiment near Nam

EF-10Bs provided critical support for early anti-SAM missions in North Vietnam. This specific aircraft (BuNo 124632) participated in one of the first US Navy *Iron Hand* strike against North Vietnamese SAM sites on 10 December 1965, crewed by Maj Don Morgan and Capt Jim Doyle (*Tailhook Association*)

Dinh. The strike destroyed two of the regiment's four SA-2 battalions for only one loss. As Doyle recalled;

'We were up there, we were in a racetrack pattern, and we had planned it so that we would always have one aircraft facing the site, jamming. On that particular mission, we had an A-4 that was hit by AAA, but he made it out to the coast and ejected. We got the site, and that was our only loss.'

As the air war over North Vietnam intensified, VMCJ-1's Whale crews became far more proficient, while at the same time dealing with a rapidly-expanding air defence threat and increasingly competent radar operators and AAA and SAM crews.

Jim Doyle explained the demands the EW mission placed on ECMOs as they worked to stay abreast of new emitters, and their locations, while on ingress and egress from their jamming tracks in North Vietnam;

'Going up there, I would be doing ELINT work. If I picked up a "Whiff" or a "Fire Can" or another fire control radar, I would go ahead and (using the "Hack system") try to pinpoint where that emitter was based upon our position. I would record the signal, I took notes on the signal, and I had to do all this ELINT work after I got back, but this was all en route to the strike area.

'When you got up to the attack area, you had to be conscious of what kind of search radar you were working, then find the fire control radars. Was a "Spoon Rest" operating? That was associated with the SA-2. Did you pick up a "Fan Song" – one of the beams of the acquisition radar? You were busy the entire time looking at your scope. You weren't looking out the window. You were sitting right there next to the pilot, and the pilot's responsibility was to keep track of where he was, so when we got back, we could recount our track going up there.'

In the EF-10B, ECMOs relied on a combination of visual representations of radar signals on an oscilloscope display and audio of live radar signals in their headsets to help analyse what types, and even models, of radars were operating in an area. As Doyle explained;

'All those audios were different. A search radar was appreciably different to a "Fan Song" radar when it came to the audio. You knew if it was a sweeping radar, where you got a blip on your indicator, then the blip was gone, then maybe ten seconds later you got another blip. From that you could get a scan rate, and you knew the thing was going around in a circle and only hitting you once every ten seconds. If you got a signal that was on you all the time, and was kind of humming and singing, you knew that was a fire control type radar.

'The "Fan Song" was very distinctive. "Fire Can" – the AAA gun radar – was also very distinctive. You just got to know what they sounded like, and you knew the frequency range you were in, so you knew where to look for a "Fire Can" or a "Fan Song", or for a "Bar Lock" search radar. It was something that you learned by doing it. As far as looking at the scope, you knew exactly what it was when it came up.'

In addition to real time audio and visual analysis, ECMOs also recorded signals intercepted for post-mission analysis. Tape analysis occurred in a purpose-built GSQ-41 ground data readout van outfitted with tape machines and oscilloscopes. The van was air-conditioned, which made it a welcome respite from the baking sun on the Da Nang flightline. The pilot participated in the analysis as well, as it was his responsibility to navigate during the entire flight and make notes of the track he flew inbound and outbound from the target. Knowing the aircraft's position at various points during a mission was critical for being able to locate the various emitters detected throughout the flight. As ECMO Wayne Whitten observed;

'We were buried in our scope doing the ECM stuff, and we depended on the pilot to know where in the hell we were and fly all of our tracks and all that.'

After a crew analysed their mission tapes, they were packaged up and sent to the Pacific Command (PACOM) ELINT Center in Fuchu, Japan, for further analysis.

The relationship between VMCJ-1 and PACOM ELINT dated back to the early days of the 'Shark Fin' missions from Iwakuni. Marine ECMOs occasionally did two-week rotations at Fuchu as on-call EF-10 subject matter experts. As a young ECMO, Hugh Tom Carter spent two weeks of his Vietnam tour at Fuchu. He recalled the high regard the analysts had for VMCJ-1;

'They thought we were gods because we sent them intelligence they could really use. The Navy VQ aircraft were what we called "garbage collectors". They'd go up, turn on their receivers and record the signals, but the analysts there in Fuchu had no idea where these had been collected. They didn't know if they were from Hainan or North Vietnam. So what we did was feed [the ELINT Center] a reliable enemy radar order of battle. It was real intelligence, and they loved it. That was all thanks to the "Hack system" and guys like Meek Kiker, "Moose" Simolin and Joe Stone.'

The admiration between PACOM ELINT analysts and VMCJ-1 ECMOs was mutual, with Carter observing;

'The great thing about it is these guys could go through and analyse the maintenance cycle of a particular site. They spent all this time looking at the signals, and after a while they could figure out which ones were down for maintenance and when. They did some amazing work, and that's all because of the quality of the tapes that we sent them.'

Just as often, VMCJ-1 received useful information from Fuchu. As Maj Jim Doyle recalled;

'We would submit an after-action report, and then they would come back and tell us whether or not our evaluation was accurate. We just called it like we saw it, and then they would go ahead and analyse the tape. That's how we knew that we had gotten a "Spoon Rest". They had come back saying that it was, in fact, a "Spoon Rest".

THREAT PROLIFERATION

The US Marine Corps had brought the EF-10B to Vietnam to counter an expanding North Vietnamese air defence network, and the proliferation of AAA guns, SAMs and radars to control both quickly validated the decision to transfer VMCJ-1 to Da Nang. Arriving in April 1965, Chuck Houseman witnessed the build-up of threat systems first-hand;

'There was an immediate increase in the radar-controlled guns. We could monitor that with the equipment we had on the aircraft. More of those were cropping up because they could bring those things in from China and Russia via Haiphong harbour, where we were not allowed to touch them. That was another political issue. So the AAA guns were increasing. I was there on a mission, I think in late June 1965, when somebody, I think it was my wingman, said "What the hell is that over there at 'ten o'clock'?", and it looked like a telephone pole flying straight up. That was our first SA-2, and it was on the hunt. It was maybe about ten miles away, but it was big enough that you could see it. We reported it, and they said, "We've gotten several reports, and those things are cropping up".

'The next thing you know, it's like the Cuban Missile Crisis. Those ships came in and loaded them up with those SA-2s, and they had all the time in the world to truck those things wherever they needed them – they'd set them up at night and they'd camouflage them and you'd never know where they were at.'

By 1965, the US Marine Corps' remaining EF-10Bs were tired and old, with nearly obsolete EW gear, but pilots and ECMOs did the best they could, providing what proved to be stopgap jamming and SAM warning for the USAF between spring 1965 and spring 1966. These missions proved to be the second time in the Skyknight's lifespan that the USAF had relied on US Marine Corps 'Whales' to keep its aircraft safe over communist territory (*Warren Thompson Collection*)

For as much of an increase as Houseman and the other aircrews in the initial cadre noticed, the pilots and ECMOs who relieved them in October 1965 saw exponential growth in the number of threat systems in North Vietnam. Wayne Whitten explained to the author;

'The SAM network was expanding bigtime. That was a game-changer all over. The AAA was the same thing. My God, the number of new sites popping up was staggering. The scopes got increasingly cluttered. It got more difficult because there were all these intertwined signals that were in there. From the fall of 1965 through the next nine months, the signal level out there at least doubled, maybe tripled. When you were having major strikes, the Air Force would be getting stuff on one side, with the Navy on the other, so the whole air defence network was all lit up when that was happening. It was increasingly difficult to sort out which signals went with the one threat in the target area that you were trying to cover.'

The proliferation of 'Fan Song' radars for SA-2 guidance proved the most troublesome, as strikes began attacking targets that fell within overlapping SAM coverage rings. As Whitten recalled;

'It was increasingly difficult to sort through that to find THE "Fan Song" we needed to jam. There'd be two or three of them up at once, and we were trying to match the "green worms" on the scope with the sound. The most pronounced was the "Fan Song's" scan. It literally sounded like a bag of rattlesnakes, it would absolutely catch your attention. When that thing went off, boy, you knew it, you knew they were tracking us.'

In the face of a rapidly proliferating air defence network, and with the far more capable Grumman EA-6A delayed by developmental and budgetary issues until the autumn of 1966, VMCJ-1's EF-10B crews persisted, providing the best support they could with out-of-date equipment. WO Jerry O'Brien summed up VMCJ-1's efforts during this period, writing;

'What we could do was to go in and jam and drop chaff in an incredibly intense antiaircraft environment in order to confuse the enemy for very short periods of time. Possibly, hopefully, it would be long enough to complete the mission, bring as many men home as possible and totally devastate the key points in the enemy's supply system.'

Additionally, as Whitten explained, the SAM operators still lacked mastery of the SA-2;

'I think we enjoyed some success against the SA-2 simply because SAMs were very new then to the Vietnamese – they were still being trained on them by the Russians. Where I think we did well was throwing in an element of confusion [to the enemy's target-tracking picture] that saved some of our guys. The combination there in early 1966 was that their ineptitude and our limitations were well matched up.'

With the proliferation of AAA and SAM sites in North Vietnam, the Skyknight's capacity to jam all emitters threatening the strike packages waned. In the period between autumn 1965 and mid-1966, when US Navy and USAF aircraft began carrying missile launch and radar warning receivers (RWRs), the 'Whale' was an increasingly important source of SAM warnings. As Whitten recalled;

'I really think the most significant contribution the "Whales" made early on was providing threat warning to the strike and recce aircraft that did not have radar warning devices. For almost the whole year that we

'BLIND BAT' MISSIONS

Concurrent with *Rolling Thunder*, the USAF ran an interdiction campaign over Laos and Cambodia, seeking out and destroying targets along the Ho Chi Minh Trail – the network of infiltration routes from North Vietnam, through Laos and Cambodia into South Vietnam. As in Korea, the communists quickly learned that moving troops and supplies down the Trail in broad daylight left truck convoys, bicycle porters and elephant trains open to air attack. As the North Vietnamese shifted to night movement down the Trail, the USAF experimented with innovative means of detecting communist activity in the dark.

Project 'Blind Bat' was one of the early attempts to deny the North Vietnamese the cover of darkness. Beginning in early 1966, 'Blind Bat' involved Lockheed C-130 Hercules transports outfitted with a large night observation device (NOD) in one of the paratroop doors to detect targets at night and a forward air controller (FAC) on board to direct strike aircraft to drop ordnance on the targets below. 'Blind Bat' C-130s flew with two Martin B-57 Canberras to engage targets discovered through the NOD, which was done under the light of parachute-equipped illumination flares dropped by the Hercules.

Because intelligence reports indicated the possible presence of radar-controlled AAA in Laos, the USAF requested, and received, EF-10B support, with VMCJ-1 providing one 'Whale' and one crew for every 'Blind Bat' mission. To deny gunners on the ground visual acquisition of the C-130, the Canberras or the Skyknight, all aircraft in the package flew blacked-out, with only the Hercules having a single dim formation light atop the fuselage. While the FAC on board the C-130 could see in the dark through the NOD, every pilot in the gaggle relied solely on unaided vision to remain in formation.

Despite the dangers of flying over North Vietnam, EF-10 crews who flew 'Blind Bat' missions unanimously agreed they were far more hazardous than *Rolling Thunder* strikes. Recounting his own 'Blind Bat' experiences, Chuck Houseman said;

'It was hairy. We'd take off behind the C-130 and fly on their wing, then slowly move over to the Trail. As soon as it got dark, they were hoping that the trucks carrying supplies on the Ho Chi Minh Trail would be moving and using some form of light to see where they were going, just enough to where the C-130 could drop a few flares, light it up, and those Air Force B-57s would throw some bombs on the bunch. If they hit near a truck that was filled with ammunition, there were quite the fireworks. That didn't help our visual acuity, as when that flash hit, it killed our night vision.

'It was bad enough flying at night and sitting slightly off to the side and above the C-130, and it's like he's there, but it's black as ink, and there's just one little light on top of the C-130 fuselage – very much vertigo-inducing, I might add – and the light is dimmer than the light on your flashlight. We had to fly, and of course if he made a turn, he had to talk to us and let us know if he was going to turn to starboard or port. I'm glad I didn't have to do it more than two or three times. We hated the hell out of it because it was just asking for a damned accident.'

'KILLER WHALE'

During the conversion from the F3D-2 to the F3D-2Q/EF-10B, the US Marine Corps elected to keep two of the type's four M2 20 mm cannon. With no need for the guns during the late 1950s and early 1960s (the US State Department having assured the Soviets the 'Shark Fin' flights were unarmed), maintenance on the guns lapsed. However, by mid-1965, the squadron's ordnance shop had made the guns fully operable once again, and EF-10Bs routinely flew with loaded cannon as last-ditch defensive options.

With the limited number of 'Whales' in Vietnam, and the importance of the EW mission, EF-10 crews were restricted from using the cannon offensively, although that did not stop one pilot from doing so.

The first known instance of a Skyknight crew firing the guns in anger in Vietnam was on 23 December 1965. 1Lt Ken Crouch and his ECMO 'Woody' Wood had launched on a mission to support a US Navy strike in the Thanh Hoa area. The mission quickly fell apart when Crouch's wingman aborted and the US Navy cancelled the entire strike.

On the flight back to Da Nang, Wood detected a signal emitting from Tiger Island, a small North Vietnamese-held island a few miles off the coast just north of the DMZ. Curious, Crouch descended for a closer look. As the Skyknight headed for a hill on the island that would be the most obvious place to position a radar, Crouch and Wood noticed tracers coming directly toward the aircraft. Crouch aimed at the approximate source of the tracers and returned fire with the twin 20 mm cannon, taking a hit while pulling off-target. Despite a minor shudder, Crouch decided to make another pass, expending the rest of his ammunition, before heading back to Da Nang with smoke trailing from the left wing.

As the crew later learned, a 37 mm AAA round had penetrated the left wing and destroyed the tyre, which fell into the ocean when Crouch lowered the landing gear. While he successfully made an arrested landing with only the right main and nose gear at Da Nang, the incident illustrated why EF-10 crews were restricted from strafing ground targets. With just six aircraft to provide jamming and ECM support over North Vietnam, the 'Whale' was just too valuable to risk losing in ground attack missions that other aircraft were far better suited to.

Three months later, Crouch fired the 'Whale's' guns once again, this time responding to a USAF FAC's urgent request for any available aircraft to assist with a troops-in-contact firefight on 1 March 1966. Crouch made multiple strafing passes, breaking up the enemy attack, and was credited by the FAC with two enemy killed in action. Upon returning to Da Nang, Crouch and his ECMO on that mission, Capt Jim Gazzale, remained quiet about the incident, as the former's previous disregard for the restriction on strafing did not endear him to his superiors.

As it was, 1st MAW leadership received an after-action report from the USAF FAC praising the 'Whale' crew that responded to his request and engaged the enemy to good effect, and Crouch and Gazzale found themselves in hot water. As Wayne Whitten recalled;

'The powers that be found out about it and said "What? Who in the hell did that? How did that come about?" So they had to go up and stand tall before the Wing G-3 [Operations officer], a Colonel, and got their asses chewed. Just as they were walking out the door, he said "And, by the way, boys, it was sure nice to hear that old 'Willie' got a piece of the action".'

Illegal as it was, the incident proved to be the final time a Skyknight's guns were fired in anger.

VMCJ-1 suffered a third EF-10B loss on 24 March 1967 when Capt Joseph P Murphy and 2Lt Walter Albright failed to return to Da Nang following a post-maintenance test flight, and they were presumed to have gone down in the South China Sea.

In the years between the Korean War and the Vietnam War, US Marine Corps Skyknights retained the escape chute for emergency egress. Of the five EF-10s VMCJ-1 lost during the Vietnam War, none involved a pilot or ECMO bailing out successfully. For emergencies under 2000 ft, Skyknight crews generally accepted that there was little chance of surviving a bailout, as the time needed to unstrap from one's seat, slide through the chute and open the parachute left little time for a survivable descent.

POL STRIKES AND OTHER MISSIONS

Prussian general and military theorist Carl von Clausewitz wrote that war is a 'continuation of politics by other means', and this was especially true of Operation *Rolling Thunder*. Devised by the Johnson Administration as a means of pressuring North Vietnam's leadership to the negotiating table to end the war, *Rolling Thunder* employed a gradualist approach, with Johnson authorising targets of increasing strategic importance in the face of continued North Vietnamese intransigence.

In April 1966, Johnson removed the restriction on targeting North Vietnam's petroleum, oil and lubricants (POL) infrastructure, with the US Navy and USAF capitalising on that with a series of strikes during the summer months. The two services made simultaneous strikes against POL facilities on 29 June, sending a combined 46 aircraft against targets near Hanoi and Haiphong – up to that point, the closest strikes to either city. Jim Doyle flew as an ECMO supporting the US Navy strike near Haiphong;

'My pilot flying that day was Marty Brush. It was two crews, it was me and Brush, and the other ECMO was Jim Gazzale, but I don't know who the pilot was. We were up there circling over the water. It was just a beautiful day. The thing I remember most about it was it was so clear. We were sitting there off the coast, and in the target area we moved in much closer than we were supposed to. We could see the missiles coming of the pads there at the mouth of the bay going into Haiphong. We escorted that mission and got a "you did good" from the Navy. That particular mission was a big one for us, with those POL facilities being right outside of Haiphong. That was the mission that was cited when VMCJ-1 got a Navy Unit Commendation.'

'Whales' continued to provide EW assistance for strikes on POL facilities through July, with the VMCJ-1 Command Chronology noting;

'VMCJ-1 provided active ECM support and missile warning for the highly successful Haiphong POL strike and the re-strike on 14 July, as well as the succeeding series of Navy POL strikes in the Haiphong and Thanh Hoa areas. This series of strikes in July included the Do Son POL on 3 July,

Thanh Hoa POL on 6 July, Cat Bi [Haiphog] POL on 8 July, Nam Dinh POL on 14 July, Thai Bunch on 11 July and Haiphong Bomb Damage Assessment [BDA] photo-recce on 2 July. An increased use was made of the ALQ-31 pod containing two S-Band ALT-19 barrage jammers. They were used successfully to interfere with and suppress fire control [gun laying] radar emitters in high emitter concentrations. They were also used against the SAM-associated radar, the "Fan Song".'

In addition to covering US Navy daylight strikes, VMCJ-1's EF-10Bs also flew night missions in support of US Navy (and, later, US Marine Corps) A-6 Intruders. Wayne Whitten flew several such missions during his tour;

'They did mostly night flying, usually a pair of A-6s, although occasionally just one. They did their thing, and we supported them quite well. I think we did a better job with them. The combination of their capabilities, it being night and us being able to better position ourselves meant we did quite well supporting those missions.'

Although the squadron's focus had by now shifted primarily to the US Navy, VMCJ-1 still supported the occasional USAF mission, including some interesting ones that Whitten recalled participating in;

'We also flew ECM escorts for USAF C-130s and sometimes F-4s on leaflet drops over North Vietnam. I was briefed to fly one on Christmas eve of 1965 that was to drop toys with the leaflets up near Hanoi when no other flights were scheduled. Luckily someone up the chain of command cancelled that mission as we were manning up to fly!'

DMZ PATROLS

In August 1966, VMCJ-1 put its 'Whales' to work on a mission it would fly through to the final Skyknight sorties of the war more than three years later – passive electronic surveillance of the area north of the DMZ. These patrols were in response to suspicion that the North Vietnamese were moving radar systems into the area. The US Marine Corps teamed up with the US Navy to monitor the DMZ for any emissions associated with air defence systems, with US Navy EA-3 Skywarriors from VQ-1 flying the day shift from 0600 to 1800 hrs, while VMCJ-1 flew the 1800 to 0600 hrs night shift.

The DMZ mission was mostly passive, with pilots flying racetrack orbits either between the coast and the Laotian border or a north-south track off the coast perpendicular to the DMZ while the ECMO monitored his gear for any hostile emissions. ECMO Capt Terry Miner summed up the feelings of many 'Whale' crews assigned DMZ sorties;

'Half our missions were DMZ patrols. Talk about boring. I kept one eye on the equipment and one eye on my kneepad as I wrote home during that time. Two o'clock in the morning for three hours flying back and forth across the DMZ looking for guys who might or might not be awake. Nothing exciting ever happened on those missions.'

However, something did happen on one of those missions, when, shortly after the squadron began flying the patrols, EF-10B crews detected emissions from a 'Cross Slot' early warning radar just two miles north of the DMZ. The discovery of this radar initiated a series of events that included one of the few operational uses of the EF-10B's K-17 camera, and led to the eventual destruction of the radar. In his book *Silent Heroes*, which chronicles the history of US Marine Corps electronic warfare, Wayne Whitten recounts VMCJ-1's efforts to find, fix and facilitate the finishing off of this audaciously-placed radar;

'For several nights running, my fellow ECMOs and I intercepted and reported this new night owl radar, as it was usually all we picked up most nights, and no one reported receiving emissions from it during the daytime. Capt Cliff Jackson, a 1st MAW EWO, noted these intercepts in his daily brief to the 1st MAW Commanding General and his staff, and it quickly became a topic of speculation as to its purpose and threat potential. As a result, Cliff was directed to task us to get a targetable location, and, according to the records, we delivered less than four hours later!

'That night, two EF-10Bs were fragged to cooperatively get a good fix. CWO-3 Daryl Cook and I (then a First Lieutnant) were the ECMOs on that mission. Arriving on station, we found our adversary was on the air; the challenge was on. Our pilots worked hard to keep accurate aircraft positions as Daryl and I took several DF [direction-finding] cuts from all aspect angles. We then did some homing runs, with our position at station passage marked by the USAF 'Sky Spot' tracking radar located south of the DMZ.'

While working to fix the location of the 'Cross Slot', the two Skyknights drew the attention of a flight of USAF F-4C Phantom IIs working in the area and looking for something to bomb. The ECMOs passed along the approximate coordinates of the radar site, and the F-4 crews dropped multiple cluster bombs on the area, after which the emissions from the radar ceased. Whether the radar was struck and repaired or simply taken off-air once bombs started falling, two nights later, the site was back in business. With the site clearly of importance to the North Vietnamese, the Commanding General of 1st MAW ordered it destroyed.

Targeting imagery was needed to plan a strike, but the USAF-driven politics of which service could fly their aircraft where restricted the US Marine Corps from sending photo-reconnaissance jets north of the DMZ. This meant VMCJ-1's RF-8A Crusaders could not fly the photo mission. However, unbeknownst to the USAF, the EF-10 retained a reconnaissance camera, and Maj Jim Doyle, the squadron's liaison officer at Seventh Air Force in Saigon, 'fragged' a notional ELINT mission north of the border, with the actual purpose being to photograph the suspected location of the 'Cross Slot'. Whitten, who flew the photo mission as ECMO with 1Lt Gail Sublett as his pilot, recalled;

'Our instructions were to make only one photo pass at about 8000–10,000 ft as I recall over the suspect area, and we did that with the old K-17 camera chugging along. Afterwards, "Subs" and I agreed that with it being a clear day, we stood a good chance of picking up the radar site if we made a low-level visual run. The next thing I knew we were looking at a bunch of (automatic weapons and) AAA up front and personnel with lots of scared natives running from this new Yankee pirate "attack" plane.

'On our second pass we took a hit that sounded like an artillery shell exploding, and as "Subs" pulled up and away we decided that, discretion being the better part of valour, we ought to return to base with our prize film. Everyone gathered around on the flightline to gawk at a fist-sized hole in the nose cone while the photo shop downloaded the film and ran off to process it. Needless to say, there were some hard questions being asked as to how we got hit by an automatic weapon round at the directed altitude.

'We were saved from further inquisition by our skipper, Maj "Pa" Tucker, by a call from Jim Doyle, tasking us to get the film down to Seventh Air Force ASAP. The Air Force wanted their Intelligence pros to analyse it, and they also wanted the flight crew to come down for a debrief. So "Subs" and I jumped in another "Whale" and went off to Saigon with the film. Turns out we had indeed got the radar on film, albeit a bit blurry.

'Somehow, a couple of days later, we got to "frag" our RF-8As for a follow up to get a nice targeting image, and Capt Mike Gering, our S-3 [Operations officer] and another of our pilots did the honours, not only confirming the radar, but numerous lucrative targets around it.'

Destruction of the 'Cross Slot' site fell on the shoulders of MAG-11 at Da Nang. As Whitten told the author;

'That was all MAG-11, it was an all-Marine show. We picked up the "Cross Slot" with the F-10, got its location, got permission to go fly that photo mission, and then the Marines followed up with the RF-8s Seventh Air Force to go and get targeting-quality images. Then the Marine F-4s and F-8s went in and hit them, then we did the BDA. Every bit of that was done by our group up in North Vietnam. It was just across the DMZ there, but it was a Marine Corps first – no Navy, no Air Force. And the "Whale" was right at the heart of it, looking at it both ways, getting both the EW side and the target photos.'

EA-6A ARRIVES AT DA NANG

After significant developmental delays, the first six EA-6A 'Electric' Intruders arrived at Da Nang on 28 October 1966. The new aircraft brought appreciably more to the EW mission than the EF-10B, including ejection seats, air refuelling capability, a powerful new receiver suite, greater speed and manoeuvrability and seven external hardpoints, allowing a single aircraft to carry a robust mix of jamming pods, chaff dispensers and drop tanks. Given the proliferation of radar-guided threat systems in North Vietnam, the 'Electric' Intruders arrived not a moment too soon.

While the type would eventually bear the brunt of the EW mission over North Vietnam, the EA-6A was a new aircraft with advanced avionics, which, along with increased capabilities, brought more maintenance and readiness headaches. While undeniably more capable than the EF-10, the EA-6A was far harder to keep mission-ready. As a result, the old 'Whales' soldiered on while the EA-6A was still finding its footing.

The introduction of six EA-6As doubled VMCJ-1's ECM combat potential, which the US Navy took advantage of during a series of Alpha Strikes in December 1966. These strikes – one on the night of 2–3 December and another on the night of 13–14 December – both involved nine VMCJ-1 EW aircraft (six EF-10Bs and three EA-6As). The VMCJ-1 Command Chronology recorded these missions as follows;

'The strikes conducted on 2–3 December, code word "Chivas Regal", marked another first for VMCJ-1. The nine aircraft that were launched on extremely short notice to provide maximum support as requested by

CTF [Commander of Task Force] 77 formed the largest combat ECM force in the history of the Marine Corps. These included three EA-6As and six EF-10Bs lead by the Commanding Officer, Lt Col W B Fleming.

'Again, on 13–14 December, VMCJ-1 responded to the major strikes, code word "Rusty Nail Alpha" and "Bravo", with the same effort. As a direct result of the support of "Chivas Regal" and "Rusty Nail", the Commanding Officer of VMCJ-1 received a letter of appreciation from the Commanding General, 1st MAW for a job "well done". Also quoted in the letter were extracts from [CTF 77] RADM [David] Richardson's message to the Commanding General, 1st MAW expressing his appreciation for "The responsiveness and outstanding performance of VMCJ-1 in support of CTF 77 operations" during these major strike efforts.'

Tactics employed during these missions remained focused on keeping the EF-10s out of the North Vietnamese SAM rings. Capt Terry Miner, an ECMO with the squadron during this period, explained;

'The tactic was to remain 20 miles offshore, which was the range of the real threat, which was the SA-2 at that time. Our objective – in both the F-10 and the EA-6 – was to fly at about 20,000 to 25,000 ft on a racetrack pattern in coordination with strike aircraft that were coming mostly from Navy carriers, but from the Air Force also from a variety of bases in Thailand.

'In the majority of cases, but not all, we would sit in a racetrack pattern aimed at a 30- to 50-mile track inbound to wherever the target might have been designated, because aircraft were going in to strike whatever the target was. If we had dual aircraft, one of us was headed inbound as the other was headed outbound so we could maintain some weapons against the radars that were controlling the SA-2s at that time.'

During this period, one 'Whale' (BuNo 125793) sustained a hit from AAA, puncturing the centre fuel cell and damaging a flap cable, with the pilot managing a safe recovery at Da Nang.

While the EA-6A was bedded in, 'Whales' continued to undertake routine DMZ patrols throughout 1967 and into 1968. VMCJ-1 used

With delivery delayed more than a year due to development problems, the EA-6A 'Electric Intruder' – the intended replacement for the EF-10B – finally arrived at Da Nang in October 1966. Although the EA-6A outperformed the EF-10 by nearly every metric, the aircraft suffered from poor readiness rates for its first two years in operation. During 1967–68, VMCJ-1 was regularly forced to schedule mixed flights of EA-6As and EF-10Bs to ensure the US Navy or USAF still had jamming support on station should the 'Electric Intruder' be forced to abort for any reason (*MCARA*) the veteran jets to not only provide passive surveillance of threat systems north of the DMZ, but to also actively jam the emitters threatening aircraft operating in or transiting through the area. As senior EWO at the time, Maj Len Ingram scheduled the DMZ flights;

'The guys that were exclusively assigned to the F-10 or were only minimally-trained in the EA-6 typically got to fly the DMZ trips, with three hours on station. It took just 15 to 20 minutes to reach there from Da Nang, so you ended up with a roughly three-and-a-half-hour flight. The ECMO had his choice of whether to fly north-south over the water along the DMZ or you could actually fly east-west, parallel to the DMZ. The difficulty, particularly during daytime activities while flying east-west, was the frequent presence of artillery fire being shot across the DMZ from South Vietnam. But the ECMOs had a choice.

'Occasionally, just to vary the routine, some of us would fly that east-west route. At its western end, you were over the Trail, the A Shau Valley and the border with Laos. So we flew over the A Shau Valley, and I can tell you that it was an ugly-looking place. I had only been over there two or three times. Generally, I stayed out over the ocean because we couldn't ever be certain where the [SAM] sites were between the DMZ and as far north as Vinh.

'They had a 20-mile range with the SA-2s, so they could go quite a way north and still be able to address aircraft, particularly those coming in from the Navy – if the latter got precluded from dropping up north, they frequently came down south to see if the Marines needed CAS, and they would enter North Vietnam on their way to the Marines or Army site that needed a dump.'

Despite paying increased attention to the DMZ area, throughout 1967, the primary mission for VMCJ-1's 'Whales' remained active ECM support for US Navy strikes on North Vietnam. Threat summaries in the VMCJ-1 command chronologies for October 1966 and October 1967 demonstrate just how much radar-guided threats in North Vietnam had proliferated. In October 1966, the squadron jammed 165 'Fire Cans' and 34 'Fan Songs'. A year later, those figures rose to 630 'Fire Cans' and 259 'Fan Songs' jammed. Reflecting on this dramatic increase, 'Al' Olsen told the author;

'During my tour the threat environment up north was tremendous. I never flew over Berlin during World War 2, but I have read that the flak was more extensive over Hanoi than Berlin. We were required to log as many threat frequencies as we could during those support missions. Sometimes, it seemed like every threat radar in the world was active up there. During those support missions I was busier than a one-legged man in an ass-kicking contest. It was difficult to log anything because you were so busy working against enemy radars. I can recall logging as many as 18–20 "Whiffs" or "Fire Cans" [one frequency] and a half-dozen "Fan Songs" [two frequencies].

'The best way to handle that many threats was to concentrate on radars shifting into high PRF [pulse rate frequency]. That was the best indication that a threat radar was locked on one of our birds and about to fire guns or launch missiles.'

In a US Marine Corps oral history interview in October 1967, ECMO 1Lt Lou White explained the general procedure for mitigating these expanding threats;

'The squadron is ordered for this daily by CTF 77, the order giving the target, the location of the target, coast-in and coast-out coordinates, times, callsigns, frequencies and all other coordinating instructions. The lead operator in the flight then determines the electronic countermeasure initial point based on ingress and egress headings and distances.

'Generally, if the target is on the coast, we orbit so as to keep abeam of the strike group, providing jamming all the way to the target and back out. If the target is further inland, we orbit so as to be nearly at right angles to the strike heading, covering the target area with our jammers at all times. We normally have two aircraft on station, splitting the frequency spectrum of the "Whiff", "Fire Can" and "Fan Song" radars.

'One aircraft covers the portion of the spectrum where most "Fire Cans" are, and one aircraft where a few "Fire Cans" and all of the "Fan Songs" are to be found. Our aircraft remain on station until all the strike aircraft are reported back out over the water and out of the AAA or SAM track.'

CHASING GHOSTS REDUX

In an incident reminiscent of the early NCAP sorties in Korea, an EF-10B crew was vectored against a bogey during a DMZ patrol in terrible weather. Maj Len Ingraham, the ECMO on the 30 December 1967 mission, recalled;

'I'm not certain to this day whether the Air Force was fooling with us or not, but we supposedly had a bogey coming south from North Vietnam at night – it was during a midnight run on the DMZ. It was really miserable weather – cloudy, rainy, all that kind of crap – but they had a bogey coming down from the north into the Dong Ha area.

'When we called on station, the pilot would typically notify the controller we had 300 rounds of 20 "Mike-Mike". The Air Force knew that, and they were the controllers for the DMZ mission. They brought us down and flew us around right in the middle of the clag for about an hour, giving us vectors toward this bogey, and we were supposed to shoot him. No kidding. [1Lt Bill] Kogerman was my pilot for that flight, and we had opportunities at several reunions to discuss the situation. We still

In addition to flying the EF-10B and the EA-6A that replaced it in Vietnam, VMCJ-1 also employed the RF-8A Crusader and – seen here – the RF-4B Phantom II in the photo-reconnaissance role. Unlike the Skyknights, which regularly flew ECM missions over North Vietnam, VMCJ-1's reconnaissance aircraft operated primarily over South Vietnam (*Warren Thompson Collection*)

can't figure out whether or not the Air Force was messing with the Marines, because all of a sudden the bogey disappeared after they had been fooling around for an hour or so.'

Seventeen days later, on 16 January 1968, the US Marine Corps lost a fourth EF-10B when Capt Dave Moreland and 1Lt Paul Gee did not return from a night mission. Capt Charles 'Dean' Percival, an ECMO who had only weeks before had to identify the body of a squadronmate killed in an ejection accident during an RF-4B landing mishap, offered the following brief insight during an oral history interview in late 1968;

'In the middle of January, we lost two more buddies of mine. Dave Moreland and Paul Gee went out and just never came back. I don't know, maybe it's a little easier to take that way because they just disappeared.'

'SUPER WHALES' ARRIVE

In August 1967, with the EA-6A continuing to struggle with low readiness rates, the US Marine Corps initiated an upgrade programme for its remaining EF-10Bs. Under Airframe Change (AFC) 199, the modification added an APR-33 broadband threat receiver, ALR-27 missile launch warning receiver and a panoramic display window on the ECMO's station that showed the entire spectrum of hostile radar frequencies.

This combination of the new receiver and display made detecting and identifying threat emitters far easier than with the 1955-vintage equipment, where ECMOs had to switch between tuners and rotate dials to find specific frequencies, much in the same way older AM/FM radios worked. ECMO 1Lt Hugh Tom Carter explained;

'In the original "Whale", everything was mechanical, all analogue, and that was a problem. If you wanted to change receivers, you had to go down and literally re-tune your counter. It was horribly inefficient. With the "Super Whale", they put this open-end receiver in a heads-up position right in front of you, and you had a linear oscilloscope as well, so the combination of the two meant you could see both the missile control and the fire control radar spectrum at one time. This meant you could instantly do a SAM alert. It was great. There were a lot of other changes to the "Super Whale", but that was the main thing.'

Development of the 'Super Whale' – as AFC 199 aircraft came to be known – involved numerous VMCJ veterans, with pilot Art Bloomer and ECMO 'Duke' Steinken conducting test flights at NAS Patuxent River, in Maryland, while trialling the new radio suite, and ECMO Capt Paul Wheeler directing testing of the new ECM fit at the Naval Air Missile Test Center at NAS Point Mugu, in California. The programme also included various IFF and avionics upgrades.

Additionally, the modifications added a small semi-conical radome on the belly of the aircraft between the engine exhausts that housed a steerable jammer. However, the Marines seldom used the jammer, for VMCJ-1's mission shifted almost exclusively to passive ECM along the DMZ shortly after the first 'Super Whales' arrived at Da Nang on 26 February 1968.

The modified aircraft reached the frontline just as *Rolling Thunder* was approaching its end. On 31 March, President Johnson announced a halt to all bombing north of the 19th parallel, although the US Navy and USAF

continued strikes against Hanoi and Haiphong (both north of the 20th parallel) through to 1 November, when a complete halt on strikes on North Vietnam came into effect. Capt 'Al' Olsen flew one of these late *Rolling Thunder* support missions, and recounted his experience to a Marine oral historian. The account is illuminating in that Olsen mentions several of the systems failures 'Whale' crews were experiencing due to the aircraft's age;

'Myself and Capt Moran were scheduled to fly in support of Navy aircraft with targets in Hanoi and Haiphong. We were scheduled with two other aircraft, one EF-10 and one EA-6, and we were scheduled in an EF-10 too. The crew of the other EF-10 was Maj Stein and Capt Hawkes, and I don't recall the crew of the EA-6 [pilot Will Jackson, ECMO Len Ingram]. The EA-6 aborted the mission in the chocks and never took off. All three crews briefed the mission before we came down to the flightline, and we had briefed that if one or two of the aircraft had gone down in the chocks or gone down after getting airborne, the other one or two birds left would alter their racetrack pattern off the coast and cover the complete mission.

'After we got airborne, Capt Hawkes and I talked on squadron common frequency, and he informed me that the EA-6 had gone down in the chocks just prior to take-off, so we decided to take the pre-arranged racetrack patterns that we'd briefed. The one that I covered was the pattern just off Haiphong entrance, 20 miles off the coast. Capt Hawkes and Maj Stein were about 40 miles south of my position flying the same type of pattern 20 miles off the coast to cover the Navy attack aircraft when they came off their target.

'As soon as we got airborne and checked in with "Vice Squad" [an air traffic control agency in northern South Vietnam], it was determined that the nav aids in our aircraft were down, the ICS [intercommunications system] was down and partial instrument lights were down. This was a night hop, and although we should have turned back, we pressed on because the Navy was using its air-to-surface missiles at night for the first time, and they were watching this particular flight very closely. So I DR'ed

Identifiable by its lack of a dorsal blade antenna, addition of a VMAQ-2-style wire antenna from tail to cockpit and the semi-conical ventral radome between the exhaust nozzles, the 'Super Whale' provided VMCJ-1's ECMOs with a panoramic display showing all threat frequencies in a single window, rather than forcing them to switch between narrow-bandwidth tuners to identify specific receivers. Seen here at Da Nang in early 1968, BuNo 124620 was the first EF-10B upgraded to 'Super Whale' standard (*Tailhook Association*) [used dead reckoning for navigation – distance, speed and time] on up to the Haiphong area, with Capt Hawkes ten minutes behind us.

'We checked in with "Red Crown" [the call-sign for the fighter controllers on board a US Navy warship sailing in the Positive Identification Radar Advisory Zone off the coast of North Vietnam], informed them that our nav aids were down, and told them to hold us on a specific pattern, which we gave them, 20 miles off the coast. Capt Hawkes checked in about ten minutes later and picked up his orbit. He was having some difficulties in his aircraft as well – one of the fuel tanks on the wing was not transferring, and that would cut his time on station. The Navy aircraft entered the Haiphong area on schedule. Enemy activity increased from negligible to approximately 14 AAA radars and six SAM radars up.

'At the time that the Navy aircraft entered the area, I was busy in my own gear, and Capt Moran was monitoring UHF and receiving instructions from "Red Crown". He was also watching the area off Haiphong, and in our particular area, for other aircraft. The weather was clear that night and visibility was excellent, and he observed a tremendous amount of AAA fire. During the period of time that we were up there, he observed at least four SAMs fired, and one of the missiles was fired at us.

'About halfway through our mission, we had just reached the northern point of our orbit and he was turning south, and I was aware that there was an erratic movement of the aircraft. I came out of my own gear and I looked over at Capt Moran and hollered at him – since the ICS was down – what was he doing. He hollered back that a SAM had been launched at us and he was starting his evasive manoeuvre. I got back in my gear, and shortly thereafter – about five or six seconds – he informed me that the missile had exploded about 5000 ft below us, and he was picking up the track again.

'We got a good shot at seeing the land contours and the entrance to the harbour when he went into his evasive manoeuvre, and when we got back to the squadron, we guesstimated a plot of our position and determined that "Red Crown" was holding us ten miles off the coast, rather than 20 miles. This meant the controller was running us right through the middle of a SAM ring located at the entrance to the harbour.

'The mission was uneventful after that. Capt Moran said that he observed a great deal of AAA fire, and initially it would appear to be concentrated as though it were tracking. Then, all of a sudden, it would be very erratic and all over the sky, which was a good indication that that particular controlling radar had had its lock broken by my jamming and was no longer tracking a particular aircraft.

'"Red Crown" informed us after about 20 to 25 minutes on station that all the chicks had reported "feet wet" and all had gotten out safely. They delivered their ordnance, and I don't recall what the damage done by that ordnance was determined to be. We started to head back, using a combination of dead reckoning navigation and homing on "Panama" radar on my EW gear. Capt Hawkes and Maj Stein left at the same time we did, with approximately 1500 to 2000 lbs of fuel less than what they should have had, and they made it directly back to Da Nang.'

Of note in Olsen's account is one method EF-10 crews had of knowing their jamming was effective – AAA guns steadily tracking on a target suddenly firing erratically as the radar's lock was broken. Interviewed by the author in 2021, Olsen mentioned another means of assessing the efficacy of jamming;

'Although there is no report card in combat, I had a way of knowing how effective I was during those Navy strikes up north. When they would ask if we were on station, and received an affirmative from us, the next transmission you would hear was, "Navy 123 going feet dry with eight chicks". That meant they were crossing the coastline and heading inland. Approximately 30 minutes later you would hear, "Navy 123 going feet wet with eight chicks". That meant the eight Navy birds had entered the Hanoi complex, completed their mission and were now crossing the coastline and heading back to their ship, without any losses. Mission accomplished.'

With the bombing halt north of the 19th parallel, US air efforts focused more heavily on the route packages in southern North Vietnam and on the Ho Chi Minh Trail in Laos, particularly on choke points like the Ban Karai pass. During this period, VMCJ-1 experienced its final EF-10B loss on 17 July 1968 when 1Lt Ariel Cross and Capt Lionel Parra (in BuNo 125793) did not return after an ECM mission near the DMZ. Cross joined the squadron at around same time as Capt Dave Foss, who recalled;

'The problem when we had airplanes that got hit, most of our missions were single-aircraft operations in that timeframe. So if something happened, if you didn't get out or couldn't make radio contact, you just didn't come back at your appointed time. We had an F-10 go out, the pilot was 1Lt Ariel Cross and the countermeasures officer was Capt Lionel Parra, and they never returned. We had no idea what happened. As I recall, it was not a standard mission off the DMZ. They were feet dry in South Vietnam near the DMZ.'

Foss suggests perhaps a 57 mm AAA gun near the DMZ brought Cross and Parra down. Other aircrew have speculated on the cause of the loss, with Art Bloomer mentioning a thunderstorm and Len Ingram suspecting an unfortunate impact from an artillery round crossing the DMZ;

'We didn't always get the artillery fire mission activities, and some of the rounds, the 155 mm shells particularly, would penetrate our typical altitude, which was about 18,000 ft. I've always speculated that they got up over there in the middle of a fire mission, and the reason that they had no time to get on the radio and say anything was that they were hit by a round, and it was catastrophic.'

Bloomer's suspicion of weather as a cause of the Cross/Parra loss was not without merit. Since entering the war, the Skyknight had proven itself to be one of the most robust tactical aircraft in the US inventory when it came to surviving severe weather. VMCJ-1 aircrews demonstrated this night after night whilst flying the DMZ patrols, even during the peak of monsoon season.

'Al' Olsen recalled a mission in which a typhoon nearly brought his 'Whale' down. The typhoon had grounded all aircraft at Da Nang, and he had retired to the officers' club for a toddy. There, the squadron duty officer tapped him on the shoulder and informed him he had to fly a mission immediately, as a Marine infantry unit on the DMZ was about

EF-10B BuNo 127034 was another airframe upgraded to 'Super Whale' configuration. Initiated in August 1967, the 'Super Whale' programme aimed to provide the remaining EF-10Bs with slightly more potent EW capabilities as the veteran jets continued to fill the gaps left by low EA-6A readiness rates and developmental delays with the 'Electric Intruder's' ALQ-86 jamming pods (*Warren Thompson Collection*)

to be overrun and the A-6s preparing to provide CAS for them required ECM support. Although the all-weather EA-6A was the obvious choice for the mission, none were in an 'up' status, leaving the 'Whale' as the only option.

'So, off we go in an aircraft that was anything but all-weather', Olsen recalled. 'The flight up to our support orbit was the roughest one I ever experienced, before or after. There was thunder, lightning, heavy winds and almost total darkness. We were being thrown around the sky like a ping-pong ball. I was convinced that we would end up bailing out. However, the A-6s did their job, the Marines on the ground were saved and the only casualty was us!

'About halfway through the mission, a tremendous explosion in the nose of our bird, plus the brightest flash of light I had ever seen, occurred. All electrical power in the aircraft shut off and the cockpit went pitch black. My instant thought was that a SAM had got us. At the same time I knew it was not a missile. There were no missile sites showing on my equipment. My pilot and I were hollering at each other "What happened?", and then, just as fast as the blackout occurred, all electrical power came back on. We both immediately checked our systems, and the first thing my pilot hollered to me was the engines were still working and the aircraft was okay. My equipment also checked out okay. We continued with our mission and ultimately landed without further incident.

'While going through the hot refuelling pits, I exited the aircraft and did a walkaround. I then discovered what happened. There was a hole directly centred on the nose of our aircraft. It was about as big as a basketball. We had received a direct hit by a bolt of lightning.'

VMCJ-1 nearly lost another 'Whale', and its crew, in July 1968 when 1Lt Bill Blatter and ECMO 1Lt Terry Whalen had both engines quit while on approach to Da Nang after a pre-dawn DMZ patrol. Recounting the experience, Whalen said;

'At Pensacola, in one of the classes I was in, they were talking about a double flame-out, and I remember the instructor saying that it gets very quiet in a hurry, and guess what – it became very quiet in a hurry. When it happened, the first thing I did was turn around, look at the chute and think "Well, we gotta blow that thing". After it all happened, I realised we were low enough that it would have been "One-one-thousand, two-one-thousand SPLAT!"

'I don't remember being scared. It happened, and Bill said "Hold the flashlight". We were still in touch with ground control, and they had picked up the fact that we were losing altitude. They asked us if they should inform search and rescue, and I said "Yeah, sure". I was not terrified. I was looking over at the guy manning that airplane, and I knew deep down he was going to get it going again. And he did, as I recall, at 700 ft.

'I remember looking out the window and seeing leaves going by the airplane. We were going down, and he was calling out the altitudes, and right after 700 ft he got the airplane going again. We landed like nothing ever happened, went to the chow hall, sat there for a couple of hours, and the old timers came in and we were "yukking it up" and trying to figure out if it would have floated or not if we had gone into Da Nang Bay. I think he had the gear down, so it very likely would have flipped, but we never came to a conclusion on that.'

Several months later, Capt Dave Foss encountered every 'Whale' pilot's worst nightmare at Da Nang – an engine failure on take-off;

'I took off one day and lost an engine just after raising the landing gear. I remember it was daylight, and it must not have been a particularly warm day because I was able to get back and land the airplane without losing the drop tanks, which made people think momentarily that I was okay. We were over Da Nang city, and dropping 4000 lbs of AvGas in town would have probably been some measure of a disaster. Certainly, the tanks were big, and they'd come down through walls and everything.

'It was very dicey in making the turn to come back around and land. I had about a 100-ft-per-minute rate of climb, and we had lost the engine at about 300 or 400 ft in the air, so we really got a good look at the city out of the window. It was kind of a challenging event.'

In one of the more bizarre episodes involving the EF-10B in Vietnam, Foss flew a mission while intoxicated, being pulled from the O-Club one night and told he needed to fly;

'I'd had at least three black Russians at that point, and someone came in and said "Captain, you've got to go flying', and I replied, 'I'm intoxicated, I've had three of these things and I'm in no condition to fly". He left, then came back shortly thereafter and said "You're the only pilot we've got available, you've got to fly". I said, "This is not something you can do." VMCJ-1 in those days was a big squadron. I would guess there were 75 or 80 aircrew. I couldn't believe there wasn't a pilot, because everyone had to fly the F-10. He came back and said, "You're it". And I said "If I'm it, I'm it, but I won't do this unless I have a written order that says we know you're intoxicated and we're sending you anyway. I don't need to go out there in the vehicle and make some mistake and land gear up and have somebody tell me I'm the one at fault'.

'Somewhat unwillingly, the Operations officer – it might have been Maj Draayer, who was not particularly warm toward me in any case – reluctantly wrote something out, and I stuck it in my flight suit and away I went. I was flying with a fellow named "Moose" Simolin. He was a terrific operator – about as un-smooth and tactless as a human being could be – but excellent in the airplane. I got along okay with "Moose".

'We went flying and he watched me like a hawk. He said "Son, are you going to be okay?" And I said '"Moose", I don't know, you'd better watch me', and he replied, "You can bet on that". But we got through it and got back, and it was uneventful. I knew I was not in a condition to fly. You know when you've been drinking when things are kind of fuzzy, but we took our time and did every checklist about two or three times, but we didn't extend ourselves.

Surprisingly, Foss's story is not the only one of an EF-10 pilot flying while intoxicated. 'Al' Olsen also went up with a pilot who had imbibed a bit too much prior to a mission;

'The officers had a party one afternoon at the O-Club. I left early because I had a mission scheduled that evening. My pilot was at the party and stayed longer than me. I was waiting for him in the ready room to brief for our mission when he arrived. I smelled him before I saw him. It was obvious that he had imbibed more to drink than I had. I was in a real quandary. I was not sure that he was in any shape to fly a three-and-a-half-hour mission up north supporting a Navy strike.

'We had a long discussion in the rear of the ready room. I made it known to him that I was an unhappy camper. Finally, rather than face the repercussions from my refusing to fly with him, he convinced me that he was okay to fly the mission. I told him in no uncertain terms that I was going to watch his every move like a hawk, and if he floundered in any way I was going to be all over him. The rest of our brief, pre-flight, take-off and climb out were normal, with no problems.

'About the time I was starting to relax, I became aware that something was radically wrong in the pilot's seat. He was thrashing around and seemed to be preoccupied with something. I then noticed that somehow he had pulled both toggles on his Mae West. It was fully inflated and inhibiting his ability to see the instrument panel and fly. While flying the aircraft with one hand, he was thrashing around with the other hand trying to find the tube centred on the vest allowing you to deflate the vest or blow it up if you didn't have air bottles. He could not find it! I reached over and attempted to find it, and release the air, but I could not find it either.

'There was no way we could continue this way, especially since we were approaching our target. I took matters into my own hands. I slipped my hand under my Mae West to my survival vest and extracted my survival knife. I raised my hand up, holding the knife like it was a dagger and thrust directly at my pilot's chest. It penetrated the vest, as I expected, and the air escaped. The vest deflated, and we managed to complete the mission successfully. At our mission debrief back at the squadron, my pilot told me that when he saw my knife raise up, he thought that I was so angry at him that I was about to stab him. We both determined if he was not fully sober when he saw the knife, he certainly was after.'

NO ESCAPING THE 'SUPER WHALE'

As more EA-6As rolled off the production line and entered the VMCJ community, and as improved maintenance increased the type's mission-capable rates, the US Marine Corps began relying less on the Skyknight. With all eight of VMCJ-1's EF-10Bs being 'Super Whales' by October 1968, some aircrew began raising concerns over the potential hazard posed by the new radome that protruded from between the engine exhausts along the bottom of the aircraft. Reflecting on his concerns about the placement of the new radome, ECMO Jerry O'Brien wrote;

'The engineers thought to modify the EF-10B by installing a steerable antenna on the aircraft. Unfortunately, they chose to modify the aft radio compartment. The jammer hung down about two feet below the aircraft. It was an awkward installation and not well thought out. I refused to fly in the aircraft because the jammer dome interfered with the usual escape pattern.

'All of the movies made during tests of escapes from the EF-10B clearly showed that the crew members would tumble along the underside of the aircraft until they finally fell free. These tests were conducted at relatively low speeds. Lord only knowns what sort of pattern the bodies took at high speeds. The installation of the jamming dome placed a substantial obstacle in this escape route. One can imagine what would happen if a body struck the radome at any airspeed.

'I was made the subject of considerable ridicule around the ready room, and was accused of everything from being unpatriotic to being a coward. I had known men that had bailed out, and the only common element in all

The US Marine Corps flew its final EF-10B mission on 1 October 1969 when by Capt J J Morrissey and 1Lt Fieger undertook a DMZ patrol in this aircraft, 'Super Whale' BuNo 124645. Mundane overflights of the DMZ had been VMCJ-1's primary role with the Skyknight since President Johnson's March 1968 bombing halt had come into effect (*Warren Thompson Collection*)

EF-10B BuNo 124619 was photographed at NAS North Island between the showers in February 1969, the aircraft having been shipped back to California following its retirement by VMCJ-1. The Whale has a mission tally beneath the cockpit and a 'Snoopy' character painted onto the tail. The veteran jet was flown to the MASDC within months of its return to the US (*National Naval Aviation Museum*)

those stories told after the experience was that they remembered bumping along the bottom of the aircraft before falling free.

'The Skipper, Lt Col Merritt Dinnage, saw the logic of my complaint, and the Navy Parachute Testing Unit, which was located at NAS El Centro on the Salton Sea in California, was asked to conduct tests. The result of that testing was to ground the modified "Whale". This may have been the straw that broke the "Whale's" back, but it was time the old girl went away.'

Dave Foss concurred, telling the author, 'It would be kind to say the airplane was obsolete. As an aircraft in that timeframe, 1968–69, it was by any standard an unsatisfactory warplane'.

The withdrawal of the Skyknight from Vietnam occurred rapidly. September 1969 marked the first month since the EA-6A commenced operations with VMCJ-1 that the 'Electric Intruders' flew more missions than the EF-10Bs, logging 339.8 flight hours versus only 152.5 for the Skyknight. By the end of the month, only four 'Whales' remained on strength at Da Nang, the others being flown to Cubi Point, in the Philippines, for transportation back to the US aboard ships. The final combat sortie for the EF-10B came on 2 October 1969, when Capt J J Morrissey and 1Lt Fieger flew a DMZ patrol in BuNo 124645.

The US Marine Corps retired the Skyknight on 20 June 1970 when Col Oliver Davis – who scored the F3D's second kill in Korea – flew the last operational EF-10B from Miramar, in California, to the National Museum of the Marine Corps at Quantico, in Virginia. It remains there today, more than 50 years later, unrestored and off-display – a frustrating, if fitting, fate for an aircraft that is arguably the most unsung hero of its two major wars.

APPENDICES

COLOUR PLATES

1
F3D-1 BuNo 123767 of VMF(N)-542, MCAS El Toro, California, 1951

Having flown F7F Tigercats from Kimpo during the first year of the Korean War, VMF(N)-542 returned to the US in March 1951 to train the initial cadre of Marine Skyknight pilots at MCAS El Toro on early-production F3D-1s.

2
F3D-2 BuNo 127026 (also possibly 127020) of VMF(N)-513, K-8 (Kunsan), South Korea, 1953

Upon the jets' arrival in Japan, the US Marine Corps replaced the Glossy Sea Blue and white markings of VMF(N)-513's Skyknights with an overall flat black scheme with red low-visibility markings. Some aircraft were marked with special names, with 'WF 2' wearing the name *BLACK WIDOW* in red below the cockpit. BuNo 127026 (or possibly 127020) was lost on 14 November 1954 when it crashed into the sea off North Carolina during a night training mission. Both the pilot and RO were killed.

3
F3D-2 BuNo unknown of VMF(N)-513, K-8 (Kunsan), South Korea, April 1953

The 'Flying Nightmares' fittingly marked the number of NCAP missions each aircraft had flown with a red 'nightcap' stencil beneath the cockpit. When this aircraft was photographed in April 1953 at K-8, it was adorned with 50 such markings. Note that the jet's 150-gallon drop tanks remained Glossy Sea Blue.

4
F3D-2 BuNo 127030 of VMF(N)-513, K-3 (Pohang), South Korea, 1953

When VC-4 Det 44N departed Korea in July 1953, the detachment left its three surviving Skyknights behind at Pyongtaek for VMF(N)-513. VC-4's yellow squadron insignia can be seen peeking out from behind the upper right corner of the '9' modex on the nose of this jet. BuNo 127030 later served with VMF(AW)-542.

5
F3D-2 BuNo 125826 of VMF(N)-513, K-6 (Pyongtaek), South Korea, 1953

During May and June 1953, the 'Flying Nightmares' relocated from K-8 Kunsan to K-6 at Pyongtaek.

6
F3D-2 BuNo 127022 of VC-4 Det 44N, K-8 (Kunsan), South Korea, June 1953

In June 1953, a four-ship detachment of Skyknights from VC-4 arrived at Pyongtaek to integrate into VMF(N)-513's operations over North Korea. Having cruised to the region aboard *Lake Champlain*, the unit was rarely allowed to fly at night from the carrier, frustrating the pilots and ROs. Det 44N's OIC, Lt Jerry O'Rourke, eventually managed to convince his superiors to allow him to take the jets ashore.

7
F3D-2 BuNo 127027 of VMF(N)-513, K-3 (Pohang), South Korea, 1954

The 'Flying Nightmares' remained in South Korea after the July 1953 Armistice for ceasefire enforcement. By 1954, the Glossy Sea Blue paint on several F3Ds showed considerable wear. Of note, BuNo 127027's '12^{7}/$_{8}$' modex was superstitiously stencilled on to avoid having an 'unlucky' number 13 aircraft on the flightline. This Skyknight also wore a red star beneath the cockpit, indicating a kill. Frustratingly, the authors of the squadron's wartime command diaries never indicated which aircraft crews scored specific kills.

8
F3D-2Q BuNo 125850 of VMCJ-3, MCAS Iwakuni, Japan, 1958

Following the type's withdrawal from frontline service as a nightfighter, F3Ds found new life in the EW role. The Skyknight's spacious nose and cavernous interior allowed for fitting of off-the-shelf receiving and jamming equipment. VMCJ-3 at MCAS El Toro accepted the first of the new variant, designated F3D-2Q, in December 1956. Serving with VMCJ-3 from 1958 through to 1965, BuNo 125850 was then transferred to VMCJ-2. It was retired by the unit to the Military Aircraft Storage and Disposition Center (MASDC) at Davis-Monthan AFB, in Arizona, in 1969.

9
F3D-2Q BuNo 124596 of VMCJ-3, MCAS Iwakuni, Japan, 1958

VMCJ-3 became the first squadron to take the F3D-2Q overseas when it deployed to MCAS Iwakuni in August 1958. Squadron commander Lt Col Robert Read advocated for VMCJ-3 to fly the Skyknight along the periphery of China, North Korea and the Soviet far east as part of PARPRO. This aircraft was the second F3D-2 built, and it had been used for carrier suitability testing prior to being issued to an operational unit. BuNo 124596 was retired by VMCJ-1 to the MASDC in 1968.

10
F3D-2Q BuNo 124618 of VMCJ-2, MCAS Cherry Point, North Carolina, 1959

VMCJ-2 was the US Marine Corps' east coast F3D-2Q/F8U-1P squadron, supporting exercises and various training events along the eastern seaboard. A veteran of combat in Korea with VMF(N)-513, BuNo 124618 subsequently served with both VMCJ-1 and -3 prior to being struck off charge in June 1970. It is presently in storage as part of the National Museum of the Marine Corps collection at Quantico.

11
F3D-2Q BuNo 125809 of VMCJ-2, MCAS Cherry Point, North Carolina, 1959

Given the success of the 'Shark Fin' missions in the western Pacific, VMCJ-2 began conducting its own electronic surveillance sorties around newly-communist Cuba, playing a central role in monitoring the build-up of Soviet military equipment on the island leading up to the Cuban Missile Crisis in October 1962. This aircraft had briefly served with VMCJ-1 prior to being transferred to VMCJ-2.

12

F3D-2Q BuNo 125849 of VMCJ-1, MCAS Iwakuni, Japan, 1962

After VMCJ-3 rotated back to El Toro in 1959 at the completion of the squadron's Japan deployment, VMCJ-1 relocated from MCAS Kaneohe Bay, in Hawaii, to Iwakuni so as to maintain the 'Shark Fin' mission coverage in-theatre. The unit would fulfil this operational requirement until the spring of 1965.

13

EF-10B BuNo 125833 of VMCJ-2, MCAS Cherry Point, North Carolina, March 1964

Following the Cuban Missile Crisis, VMCJ-2 continued to fly PARPRO missions around the periphery of Cuba. The distances involved in these sorties – flown from NAS Key West – often exceeded the reliable range of the Skyknight's UHF radios, with controllers unable to reach pilots veering into Cuban airspace. VMCJ-2 modified some EF-10Bs (including this jet) with a wire antenna for a long-range HF radio so as to stay in constant contact while on these long-range missions. This aircraft was lost in a non-fatal crash at MCAS Yuma, in Arizona, on 21 October 1968 while serving with VMCJ-3.

14

EF-10B BuNo 125849 of VMCJ-1, Da Nang, South Vietnam, 1965

In response to a request for EW aircraft to escort USAF and US Navy strikes over North Vietnam, VMCJ-1 deployed to Da Nang air base in April 1965. VMCJ-1 'OpsO' Maj Jerry Mitchell and ECMO Capt 'Duke' Steinken flew BuNo 125849 on the first USAF mission to destroy SAM sites on 27 July 1965.

15

EF-10B BuNo 125793 of VMCJ-1, Da Nang, South Vietnam, August 1966

Skyknights shouldered much of the ECM burden over North Vietnam during *Rolling Thunder*. A March 1966 loss to an SA-2 forced a shift from overland tactics to operating almost exclusively over the Gulf of Tonkin and outside SAM range. This aircraft, which had previously served with VMCJ-3, was lost on 19 July 1968 when 1Lt Ariel Cross and Capt Lionel Parra disappeared while on a night DMZ mission.

16

EF-10B BuNo 127051 of VMCJ-1, Da Nang, South Vietnam, August 1966

Although capable of carrying jamming and chaff pods, the Skyknight's lack of an aerial refuelling capability forced crews to fly almost exclusively with 300-gallon drop tanks under each wing to ensure they had enough fuel to reach the Hanoi and Haiphong areas with the station time required to provide jamming with the type's nose-mounted ALT-2 system.

17

EF-10B BuNo 127051 of VMCJ-2, MCAS Cherry Point, North Carolina, May 1967

Following its return from Da Nang, BuNo 127051 was transferred to VMCJ-2 and fitted with the HF antenna modification for missions near Cuba. A second blade aerial was also installed on the upper left rear fuselage. Despite extensive efforts by the author to identify this antenna, and its function, none of the EF-10B pilots or ECMOs interviewed remembered its function. They suggested that it too was related to the intelligence collection missions near Cuba. BuNo 127051 was eventually flown by VMCJ-3 to the MASDC in June 1970.

18

EF-10B BuNo 124632 of VMCJ-1, Da Nang, South Vietnam, September 1967

As part of the modification from F3D-2 to F3D-2Q in the late 1950s, Skyknights retained two of the four M2 20 mm cannon underneath the nose. VMCJ-1 only employed the weapons on two missions of dubious legality, both involving the same pilot. However, both guns were loaded for every mission, with many pilots test-firing them en route to North Vietnam to ensure functionality. As a result, many 'Whales' returned to Da Nang with gun residue, as depicted in this profile.

19

EF-10B BuNo 125869 of VMCJ-1, Da Nang, South Vietnam, October 1967

Just as the F3D-2s in Korea wore 'nightcap' mission markings, 'Whales' in Vietnam wore red lightning bolt stencils to signify the number of jamming sorties flown by each aircraft. BuNo 125869 was involved in the daring 26 August 1966 photo-reconnaissance mission flown just a few miles north of the DMZ in search of a 'Cross Slot' radar that had been detected there.

20

EF-10B BuNo 124620 of VMCJ-1, Da Nang, South Vietnam, May 1968

In February 1968, VMCJ-1 received its first two 'Super Whales' outfitted with upgraded radios, which included deletion of the dorsal blade antenna and addition of a wire antenna (similar to the HF wires on VMAQ-2's EF-10s), a panoramic EW display showing the full range of frequencies covered by a new APR-33 broadband threat receiver and an ALR-27 missile launch warning receiver. Additionally, the 'Super Whale' featured a steerable jammer housed in a small, semi-recessed ventral radome between the two engine exhausts. BuNo 124620 was the first EF-10B modified to this standard. Retired by VMCJ-3 to the MASDC in June 1970, the aircraft was part of the now-defunct Quonset Air Museum collection in North Kingstown, Rhode Island, for a number of years.

21

EF-10B BuNo 124619 of VMCJ-1, NAS North Island, California, February 1969

Seen at North Island after being swapped out for a 'Super Whale', BuNo 124619 wears mission marks under the cockpit and a 'Snoopy' character painted onto the tail. As one of the last 'straight' EF-10Bs flown by VMCJ-1, this aircraft would have primarily undertaken the nightly DMZ patrols that became the squadron's primary mission after the end of *Rolling Thunder*. The veteran jet was flown to the MASDC within months of its return to the US.

INDEX